FAITH POWERED PROFESSION

*A woman's guide to living with faith
and values in the workplace*

Elizabeth Knox

Russell Media • Boise, Idaho

Published in Boise, Idaho by Russell Media
www.russell-media.com

This book may be purchased in bulk for educational, business, ministry, or promotional use. For information please email info@russell-media.com.
ISBN (print): 978-1-937498-32-0
ISBN (e-book): 978-1-937498-33-7
Printed in the United States of America

This book is dedicated to:

Rebecca
Emily
Abby

Adela
Esme
Daphne
Margaret

I'm honored to be in your lives
and I am excited about the women you are becoming.

Acknowledgements

There is no way to thank everyone who is involved in turning an idea into reality. Ink on paper cannot begin to express my gratitude to all who helped create this book! I'd like to thank the following people for their unique contributions:

- Rebecca Gilmore—my project manager. She has been a treasure! She kept me on track, broadened my perspective, and clarified my thoughts. Thank you for sharing your gifts with me.
- Gayle Jacobs—my partner in crime. She gave me the courage to start this book and her insight into these issues and raucous laughter kept me going!
- Jo Kadlecek—an established and successful author and my content editor. She provided the in-depth refinement I needed to finish this book. I'm so honored you came alongside me!
- Members of the Women-in-the-World Bible Studies—from the fall of 2009 and beyond. These women have been a source of knowledge and provided context around these topics. I'm especially grateful to Siri Buller, Megan Nykyforchyn-Clark, Liz Oxhorn and Angelyn Shapiro for their co-leadership and encouragement! Special thanks to Angelyn for her editing expertise!
- Meg Biallas, Molly Gill, Josie Lynne Lenney, Nathan Magnuson, and Nicole Wirth—my peer-reviewers. Their eyes and comments provided just the input I needed!
- Mom (Kathy Schloesser), Dad (Warren Schloesser), Jen

Koschmann, Julie Rutledge, Allison Davey, and Peggy Knox. These are my solid, steady, always-there-for-me people without whom I would be adrift.

- Mark Russell—CEO of Russell Media. Thank you for investing in me and this book!
- Bobby Kuber and the team at Russell Media—they have been great guides through the publishing process!
- Diane Paddison, Betsy Gray, Amanda Battaglia and the team at 4word Women. They have provided encouragement, coaching and partnership. I'm excited to be part of the ice-breaker with you!
- The Leadership at National Community Church—especially Mark Batterson, Maegan Hawley, Andy Pisciotti, Heather Zempel, and Ryan Zempel. They are a gift to our church family, making it possible for each of us to serve God with our unique skills.
- The amazing people who generously shared their stories and insight. They helped refine my thought processes, and helped me grow as a woman and an author—thank you!
- Andy Knox—my husband. I can't begin to put words around how much support he has provided. His time, support, and encouragement were never-ending and priceless. I'm so glad I married you!

FOREWORD
By Mark Batterson

One of National Community Church's (NCC) core values is that the "church should be in the middle of the marketplace." The marketplace is where people are, and we—as the Church, the Body of Christ—should meet them there.

Elizabeth Knox knows that, lives that, and encourages professional Christian women to live it themselves. I've known Elizabeth since 2004 when she started attending NCC and when I heard she was writing a book for professional Christian women, I was thrilled! There is such a need for a book like this! Many Christians pour themselves into their work, not just to make another dollar, but to make a difference. A professional who wants to influence her community for Christ needs tools and training to be successful, and perhaps just as importantly, she needs encouragement. This book provides some of that much-needed equipping and encouragement.

Professional women have been a part of the church since the earliest days. Remember Lydia of Thyatira, an early convert and first host of the church in Philippi, was a dealer in fine cloth. Other professional women like Joanna and Susanna supported Jesus' ministry out of their own means. Over the past century, and especially in recent decades, the ranks of women in professional roles have begun to soar. I am so excited Elizabeth is seeking to provide these women the tools they need to successfully live out their faith in the marketplace.

Though not theologically trained, Elizabeth is a careful researcher. She shows how the Bible and church teaching provide solid support for day-to-day spiritual "success" in the workplace. She encourages women to *get grounded*—and understand the theological foundation for thinking about work as a Christian woman. She *gets real* and addresses some of the challenging realities facing women in the workplace. And lastly, she helps women *get going*—showing them how they can integrate their faith into every aspect of their lives, including their jobs.

Another saying we have around NCC is that church is a tag-team sport: when people walk into church, they say "tag" to the pastor and the ministry team, expecting them to bring their best to the weekend services. When people walk out of church, we say "tag—you're it" and expect them to serve in their unique circle of influence. Not only did Elizabeth take our "tag" seriously by writing this book, she's equipping other women to make a difference for God in their spheres of influence. Just like the women in our church, women, whoever and wherever they are in the larger Church, can benefit from the research and experiences that Elizabeth has assembled here.

Mark Batterson,
New York Times bestselling author of *The Circle Maker*

ENDORSEMENTS

"Biblically rooted, practically oriented, and personally experienced, Knox does not simply talk about women or to women regarding their callings; rather, she issues a clear call to women to a higher level of professionalism, integrity, and excellence in the spheres they influence. For Knox, work is worship, and that means we must bring the best of ourselves. Using Scripture as her foundation and filter, she addresses the common tensions and unspoken fears faced by women who seek to represent Christ in the middle of the marketplace. She goes beyond the tired debates and outdated labels to challenge a new generation to see business as mission."

Heather Zempel,
Discipleship Pastor of National Community Church,
Author of *Sacred Roads* and *Community is Messy*

"To be honest, I wasn't sure what to expect when I read *Faith Powered Profession*. Would there be any takeaway for me as a man or is it just geared toward working women? But the takeaway is huge. This book is helpful for the career minded Christian man or woman in today's world. Knox' book will allow both men and women to better understand the women we work with as well as our wives, sisters and friends. When Knox challenges the reader to bring their faith into every aspect of their careers, it is not just a challenge for women, but for all of us. Knox' writing is both practical and inspiring."

Joel N. Clark
Author of *Awake: the book you can watch*

Christian women professionals comprise one of the fasting growing—yet most often ignored—demographic of women in the church. Elizabeth Knox aims to change that by bringing them and their world out into the open. In this visionary work, Knox dismantles the notion that work done in the business sector has secondary or derivative value (for witnessing opportunities or as a funding source for other ministries), asserting that the work has kingdom value for its own sake. The book is packed with candid discussions integrating faith with workplace realities and solid strategies for pursuing excellence. The workplace is not for the faint of heart, but calls for courage, assertiveness, and strength of faith. I hope this book gives church leaders second thoughts about overlooking this significant demographic and gives professional woman a fresh dose of courage as they serve God in the marketplace.

Carolyn Custis James, author of
The Gospel of Ruth: Loving God Enough to Break the Rules
Half the Church: Recapturing God's Global Vision for Women
www.whitbyforum.com

"What started as a conversation among her friends has become a resource for a conversation with your friends. *Faith Powered Profession* invites women to reflect deeply on questions that many face but few spend the time to answer. Elizabeth has wisely developed a book that lends itself easily to a serious conversation at the workplace, or to an ongoing gathering of women of different ages and seasons in their faith."

Stephanie Summers
CEO, Center for Public Justice

"I am thrilled to see Ms. Knox challenge Christian women to use all of their gifts and talents in the workplace, the community, the family and the church. She effectively reminds us of the truth that God has called both women and men to be His change agents in the world, equally gifting and calling us to do so, together, in every sphere of life. You will be encouraged and inspired!"

Bonnie Pruett Wurzbacher
Senior Vice President, The Coca-Cola Company (ret.)

"Why aren't there more role models of strong, smart, professional women in the church? I've been shaking my head wondering the same thing for years. Thankfully, Elizabeth Knox is stepping forward with a smart, practical and thoroughly inspiring book that I am certain will bring an enormous sigh of relief for working Christian women everywhere. No more relegating professional life of women to the Evangelical hinterlands—Knox is calling women of faith to stand proud in their calling out in the working world, making a difference, influencing for the Kingdom of God. Drawing on her own struggles and examples, Knox provides a fairly comprehensive roadmap for Christian working women to get grounded in their identity and fully integrate their Christian calling with their vocational calling."

JB Wood,
Author of *At Work as It Is In Heaven:
25 Ways to Re-imagine the Spiritual Purpose of Your Work* and
The Next Level: Essential Strategies for Breakthrough Growth

TABLE OF CONTENTS

INTRODUCTION

When I was little, I wanted to be an oceanographer. I loved whales, dolphins, and swimming, and I thought there could be no better job than studying marine animals. I still love dolphins, but that aspiration changed. Instead, I headed off to grad school and a career in the defense field, working as an intelligence analyst, a management consultant and, most recently, a program manager.

I was thrilled as a child to have so many options before me, and as I look forward from here, I'm still excited about the different paths my career may take.

Over the years, faith has become a much more important part of my life. Living out this faith in the professional world has often proved challenging, both for me and for many of my friends. We've struggled to determine how to find the right balance between our careers and our personal time, to have healthy relationships with male colleagues, and to live "above reproach" even in the littlest of things.

After one particularly trying time, I went looking for a resource for professional Christian women. But as I searched, I came up with very little. There were books for Christian women, but they were often about being a wife or a mom. A search for "Christian women leaders" turned up women who made their way into full-time ministry positions—but not Christian women who were seeking to be leaders in the working world. I asked a few older professional Christian women if they had any resources to recommend. Or did they know of someone who did? Their answers were usually, "Hmm . . . no, I've never seen a book or a Bible study on that. It would be good to have one though!"

I found there were already excellent resources for professional women and for Christians in the workplace. But I couldn't find anything that combined the two.

Working Women

Women in most cultures have been working forever – in the fields alongside their husbands, at family stores, in factories, the home, you name it. For decades, women in this country have fought so that you and I could have the opportunity to work as professionals. While there has been considerable progress toward the goals of equality and the right-to-work (women now make up 47 percent of the labor force in the United States[1]), many challenges still persist. We face the ongoing difficulty of navigating predominantly male environments, and, even now, women aren't completely sure how to advance in their careers. A recent study highlighted that while women occupy 53 percent of entry-level jobs, the number decreases to 37 percent for mid-management roles and only 26 percent for vice president or senior management positions.[2]

Yet evidence worldwide shows that a diversity of thought, leadership, and experience in an organization leads to better decision-making. Countless studies confirm how a positive relationship between the number of senior women in an organization increases the financial performance and overall health of the organization. Why, then, is it still so difficult for women to get ahead?

---

[1] Bureau of Labor Statistics, Current Population Survey, *"Table 3: Employment Status of the Civilian Noninstitutional Population by Age, Sex, and Race,"* Annual Averages 2011 (2012).

[2] Barsh, Joanna and Lareina Yee. *Changing Companies, Minds about Women.* McKinsey Quarterly. September 2011

Christian Workers

To the issue of Christians in the work place, many writers, thinkers and theologians have thankfully provided us a huge body of work laying the biblical foundation for Christians to engage in society, to help cities prosper, and to bring a godly perspective to our communities through economic engagement. People like Abraham Kuyper, Dorothy L. Sayers and Bob Briner have written on these topics for previous generations. While their works continue to provide us with much needed guidance, the topic of work is one that needs ongoing exploration and discussion, especially as our culture changes. Presenting the matter afresh to each generation exposes them to the importance of hearing God's call to the workforce. Seeing our work through a Christian lens is foundational to the ensuing challenges that await us once there: how to structure our time to reflect the priorities God has given us, and how to be a light for Him in our respective jobs.

Putting the Two Together

This book tries to combine the best of both of these topics. Some of this book is theoretical, addressing the intellectual concepts we struggle with as professional women. Some of this book is practical, trying to apply Biblical principles to our everyday lives. My overall intent is for the book to be conversational—to speak to some of the issues that address both working women and Christian workers, to tackle the overlap between the two circles. I offer some stories of my own experiences, and those of friends, as well as the many people I interviewed for the book. Since Scripture doesn't explicitly discuss the role of professional women (or men for that matter), I take what we have learned from other scriptures and try to apply it. The book is divided into three parts:

Part I: Getting Grounded—Chapters 1-4:
The theological foundation for thinking about work as a Christian woman.

Part II: Getting Real—Chapters 5-7:
Conversations about the realities of work for Christian women today.

Part III: Getting Going—Chapters 8-10:
Ensuring our faith is present in every aspect of our lives, including our jobs.

What I share on these pages is part of what I've been discovering along the way. As author Donald Miller wrote, "When we are young or immature, right theology makes us feel superior, but when we are older and more mature, a study of theology makes us feel inferior and unworthy, undeserved, and grateful." I find myself in the latter place when it comes to understanding a lived theology for work as a Christian woman and am eager to learn more as my life and career progress.

And so I offer this book in the hope of contributing that resource I went looking for, one that moves the discussion forward of what it means for us as women to explore our unique role in the family of God and our particular callings to serve the greater society.

PART I: GETTING GROUNDED
the theological foundation for thinking about work as a Christian woman

CHAPTER 1

What We Are Doing Is Important

What I urged then was a thoroughgoing revolution in our whole attitude to work. I asked that it should be looked upon, not as a necessary drudgery to be undergone for the purpose of making money, but as a way of life in which the nature of man should find its proper exercise and delight and so fulfill itself to the glory of God. That it should, in fact, be thought of as a creative activity undertaken for the love of the work itself; and that man, made in God's image, should make things, as God makes them, for the sake of doing well a thing that is well worth doing.

Dorothy L. Sayers – "Why Work?"

Several years ago a co-worker led a lunchtime bible study where we read a book by Douglas Sherman and William Hendricks entitled "Your Work Matters to God." The title struck me; maybe because I haven't always felt like my work mattered to many others besides me, let alone God. And since I couldn't steal their title, the next best way to capture this concept is to say, "What We are Doing is Important." In other words, what we do, for [at least] forty hours a week, is important to our Creator and is part of His plan.

I didn't always realize that. Much of my early spiritual growth came via a college ministry that had the stated purpose of influencing "tomorrow's world leaders for Christ." But some of the staff of that organization seemed to me to imply that God's most devoted followers would automatically go into full-time ministry. It didn't help that some of the staff from that ministry tried to convince me that I, too, was called to full-time ministry. They were wonderful people who truly served God, and were invaluable to me as a young Christian, but I believe their efforts weren't exactly helpful for someone interested in business and political science.

Many churches also promote a similar view that certain people are called to "full-time ministry." The rest of us can support those who *are* called with our paychecks and prayer. This attitude seems to suggest that we aren't the ones on the frontlines, living for God, as if our work isn't as important because it's not "full time ministry." Sermon illustrations often reinforce this, telling stories of people who are giving their whole life to Christ, highlighting the "full-time missionaries" and rarely profiling those who are trying every day to live out God's call in the professional world. To me, this communicates that full-time ministry service should be the goal of most Christians.

I want to live for God, but I have a hard time seeing myself in those stories. Do the sermon illustrations mean God doesn't need people out in the world as much as He needs pastors in the church or missionaries to the 'lost'? Does God only call people to "vocational ministry"? Part of the problem may be that we often think of our "calling" as the spiritual part of life and work as the secular. *But what if God has called you to the "secular"?*

This tension dates back at least to 300 AD when a theologian named Eusebius believed that in order to serve God fully, one must enter a sacred, rather than a secular, profession. His idea was further supported by the separation of priests and laity in the Catholic Church. Eusebius' teachings contributed to class division, relegating laity to a subordinate role to the leaders.

Church teaching on this topic since then is actually quite fascinating. Many great minds have come to different conclusions regarding the role work should have in our lives. These interpretations of Scripture regarding work continue to be debated today. Eusebius' teachings no doubt contributed to the class-division hierarchy between laity and full-time leaders in the church, making one subordinate to the other and creating a perception of prominence ever since.

But what if Eusebius was wrong? What if you can wholeheartedly serve God in a secular profession just as you can in full-time ministry? What if there is no divide between sacred work and secular work?

I'm sure Eusebius was well meaning, but I've come to believe that we don't need to be in a "sacred" full-time ministry profession in order to serve God. As a matter of fact, I believe that most of us are not called to full-time ministry; rather we are called to be salt and light to the world around us by being IN the world.

Fast forward to 1995. Bob Briner was a Christian who was also an Emmy award-winning television producer and sports manager. In his book, *Roaring Lambs*, Briner was passionate about Christians influencing the culture around them. He was frustrated with a perceived message from the Church that being called to ministry is "superior" and being out in the world is "inferior." Briner wrote that living for Christ in the professional world is "just as difficult, just as demanding as being a missionary" and he wanted the Church to encourage and support professionals as much as those called to missions.

Briner didn't say secular callings are "superior" to sacred callings, but his argument compels us to question whether there is actually a secular/sacred divide. Whether either one is superior. And if there isn't—and I don't think there is—what does that mean about how we spend our time?

There's no question the Church needs hard-working, talented people willing to live for Christ. But they are equally needed in the boardroom—and the police station, the grocery store, the non-profit organization, the county government, the classroom, the stage, and on and on.

So when pastors and church leaders don't help us integrate biblical and spiritual principles into our workplace, it often leads to a "Sunday/Monday disconnect." Yes, on Sundays we learn biblical principles, but on Mondays we aren't sure how to make them relevant to the place we spend most of our time and energy. If we come to the conclusion that work really *is* important, then we must talk about it from a biblical perspective.

Being Salt and Light—Bringing Our Skills to the World

You are the salt of the earth, you are the light of the world, (Matthew 5:13-14. NIV)

The first reason our work is important is found here in Matthew. We've all heard someone referred to as "the salt of the earth." The term gives me a picture of a sweet old woman, likely one who has recently passed away. Someone wistfully says, "Now she . . . *she* was the salt of the earth." I think what they mean is someone who is loyal, faithful, gentle, and kind. But is that what Jesus meant?

In Jesus' time, salt was highly valued. In addition to being used as compensation (that's where the phrase "worth his salt" comes from), it had many purposes—to preserve, to give flavor, and to disinfect. When Jesus called Christians to be salt, he was asking us to be a preservative for the culture, to keep the world from spoiling. He also called us to give flavor to the world—bringing hope, joy, and peace. And inherent in His call is for us to help clean the world of its ills. If you have ever gotten salt in a wound, you know it stings. But it also disinfects and acts as a purifying agent.

I think one of the most striking points is that for salt to work, it has to come in contact with the item it is trying to affect. Salt sitting on the kitchen counter does not have a preservative effect. Nor does it give flavor. It's not doing its job. Unless we as Christians interact with the world, we are failing to preserve the world and give it flavor.

To have a say in shaping the culture, we must be in the culture. And we have to be in it with excellence. Churches should be on the forefront of influencing culture; we should cultivate the best artists, the best politicians, and the best public school officials and send them out to be salt and light in the world. When we limit excellent writers who are also Christians, to write only for Christian audiences, we lose the opportunity for a strong God-fearing voice to influence the world with God's priorities.

Through this book I want to encourage you to use your professional abilities to glorify God, I want you to be salt and light right where you spend the majority of your time—at work.

Granted, it is not easy to be salt. We may face extra scrutiny because we are Christians; our opinions may be subject to skepticism from those who assume we are trying to advance a certain set of beliefs. Or if we set different boundaries than the culture in which we work, that is, boundaries about alcohol, relationships with members of the opposite sex, the hours we keep, we may be seen as someone who's not really "in-it-to-win-it."

Even so, we need Christians who are excellent in every profession, and becoming excellent in our respective fields will be tough. It's a lot easier to sit on the outside criticizing the lack of Christians in academia than it is to get our Ph.D. and become a Christian professor. It's far simpler to say there's only garbage on TV than to become an excellent producer and create better television. Why would Christians want to become professors when they feel pressure from their colleagues that their faith has no place in academics? Why would Christians become television producers when they are told that people only want programs celebrating a lack of morality? Why? Because as Christians we are called to be in the world.

According to the Salt Institute (yes, there is such a thing!) salt has more than 14,000 known uses and the world uses 240-million tons of salt a year. That is a pervasive substance! My prayer is that we, as Christians, can be just as prolific and pervasive.

Jesus' prayer in John 17 clarifies why our work matters. He said His followers are "not of the world" but that he had "sent them into the world" (paraphrase). (John 17:14, 18 NKJV) When I think of some of my own experiences, I understand a bit more of what Jesus meant. For instance, I had the opportunity to be an exchange student in Thailand. I repeated my senior year there before starting college. I was a scared, overwhelmed 17-year-old, and for the first half of the year I locked myself in my room and wrote letters home. The Internet was brand new and so I emailed friends all the time. I found the eight other westerners in my city and spent time with them whenever I could. I was physically in Thailand, but essentially 'living" in the U.S. It was an amazing experience and I learned a lot, but I really struggled to immerse myself in the culture.

Then, a few years ago, I had the opportunity to work in the Philippines at the U.S. Embassy and I was determined to do things differently than I had in Thailand. I was determined to be IN the Philippines, NOT in America. Granted, I had to be pretty intentional to do that since I was living in a western apartment building because of embassy rules and surrounded by Americans all day at work. Still, I was determined to make my personal time reflective of the culture. So I didn't hang out with the expat crew every night, and tried hard to make Filipino friends, to get to know Filipino families. I didn't stay on email all the time, even though I missed people at home.

Did I become Filipino? No. And, I wasn't supposed to—I'm still a U.S. Citizen. But as best I could, I was living my life *in* the Philippines.

In Thailand, I hung around a bunch of people like me; I didn't actually engage the culture. And sometimes, that's what we do as Christians—we spend all our time around other Christians. We forget that we're actually called to be in the world—influencing and healing and preserving. In the Philippines, I did spend time IN the Philippines. In other words, I was IN the country, but not OF the country. That's what we're supposed to do as Christians.

We need fellowship—definitely. Spending time with the Body of Christ is a wonderful thing. And we absolutely should expect our ministers and church leaders to model excellence for us, to spur us on, to lead us and develop us. I just don't think every Christian is called to use their excellent skills only within the Christian sub-culture.

Perhaps another way to think of it is to ask what your field would look like without a single Christian? Or what would it look like if all the Christians just formed their own group within each specific business area and only spent time with each other?

Work Is a Form of Worship and a Way to Be "on Mission"

The second reason our work is important is that it is a form of worship. We usually think of worship as singing, but worship is the act of taking any gifts you've been given and using them to glorify Christ. It's an act of devotion. I haven't been given musical gifts—anyone who sits in front of me in church could tell you that—but I have been given administrative gifts and management gifts and I offer those back to God.

To the right is a chart depicting a regular workday. It's essentially divided into three, eight-hour chunks. Unless you're a super-human, each of us generally needs about eight hours for sleep every night. Then you've got at least eight hours dedicated to work.

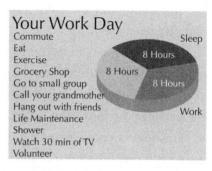

Your Work Day

Commute
Eat
Exercise
Grocery Shop
Go to small group
Call your grandmother
Hang out with friends
Life Maintenance
Shower
Watch 30 min of TV
Volunteer

Sleep
8 Hours
8 Hours
8 Hours
Work

That leaves eight hours for everything from commuting to grocery shopping to spending time with our family or friends.

And missions aren't just something we do on a short-term trip, or a service project we do with our small group, we need to factor that into the equation as well. If we think we can only worship God or live missionally in a small portion of this one section of the pie or whenever we can grab on weekends or during vacation days, I believe we are missing many opportunities. In other words, if we think we can't worship and serve God during the hours of 9-to-5, we need to rethink our purposes and roles in our work places.

I've come to see that our jobs provide great opportunities to worship God, to serve Him and others, and to advance God's kingdom with the resources we earn. Companies and businesses are the source of wealth creation. The money our paychecks generate can support social, civic or spiritual organizations. If people aren't earning incomes, who would support churches, missionaries and non-profit organizations?

An income is certainly not the only benefit of our job—though it can admittedly feel that way in a success-driven society—but it is a big one. However the actual work we do, not just the money we make from it, is a way to worship God and give back to Him.

We all know what it is like to show up on Sundays and just go through the motions. Stand up at the right times, sit down at the right times, sing when we are supposed to, be polite to the person next to us. But we know when our hearts aren't in it. We know when we're seeking the presence of God and when we are just checking a box. How many of us have gone to work just to check a box? File this report, answer those emails, attend that meeting. Doing the things we need to do to get through the day, but without putting our hearts into our job. I know I do that. I easily forget that I am called to "do my work heartily, as for the Lord and not for men" (Colossians 3:23 NKJV).

In the same way that we offer our voices as an act of worship, when we do our job well, with integrity, and when we work to ensure we are serving the interests of our customers or clients, we *are* worshiping God with the skills He's given us!

The Work Itself is Important

So our work allows us to bring God's influence and to address His priorities, to be salt and light, to be "in the world." And, it allows us to give back to Him the gifts He's given to us, offering Him our worship through our work. Lastly, the work itself is important. Work has been with us since the beginning of time—Adam and Eve worked in the garden. (Before the Fall, Adam and Eve had work to do—after the Fall is when the work got hard.) And there will be work for us to do in Heaven. God didn't intend for us to sit around doing nothing, work is an ongoing part of our stories.

Our work allows us to come in contact with the world—the world that God cared so much about, He sent Jesus into it.

There is the cerebral and white-collared work of executives; it's important that major corporations and companies be run well. But there is honor and need for godly employees at every level—even if we think we'll never "make it big." Whether we're a scientist or a home repair specialist, the work we're doing is important because we are contributing to the welfare and livelihood of society.

I'm reminded of Martin Luther King's speech defending the rights of sanitation workers to unionize and receive decent wages in 1968. He said:

> If you will judge anything here in this struggle, you're commanding that this city will respect the dignity of labor. So often we overlook the worth and significance of those who are not in professional jobs, or those who are not in the so-called big jobs. But let me say to you tonight, that whenever you are engaged in work that serves humanity, and is for the building of humanity, it has dignity, and it has worth. One day our society must come to see this. One day our society will come to respect the sanitation worker if it is to survive. For the person who picks up our garbage, in the final analysis, is

as significant as the physician. All labor has
worth.

—Martin Luther King
Memphis, TN, March 18, 1968

King was far from the only person to recognize the
contribution that good jobs provide to a society. In his book,
God is at Work, Ken Eldred notes that the European Christian
Conference asked the United States not to send missionaries,
but to send businessmen and women who could provide
opportunity for people. Businesses offer much needed goods
and services. Businesses create jobs and those jobs provide
salaries for people to support their family. As Christians we
should be running honest, responsible businesses—wouldn't
the world do better with more of those?

Meeting the material needs of people has regularly opened
the door for the gospel, but donating goods and services isn't
the only way we can meet people's needs. And it may not even
be the best way many times. Providing opportunities for people
to work, for people to have the dignity of providing for their
own families is an amazing way to communicate to others how
much God cares about them.

Through an organization called Opportunity International
I've become more familiar with microloans (small loans to
people in developing countries to help them build a business).
I had the opportunity to talk with one of their loan officers and
learned about a woman in Ghana named Mary Addo. Mary's
husband passed away and her brother-in-law told her she could
either marry him or move out of the house; she chose to move

out of the house with her four children. Through Opportunity International she joined a trust group: a weekly meeting where twenty women learn about finances and are accountable to one another. She took out a $20 loan to start a vegetable stand. She was able to repay that loan, and then she took bigger loans and repaid them until now she owns a clothing store. She is able to support herself and pay for all four of her children to go to school.

The value of people working and supporting themselves in developing countries is obvious to us. But it is just as true in developed countries. Owning, working in, or supporting businesses that provide goods the society needs, jobs and income for community members, and structure to our society is an honorable way to work for the Lord.

Consider the message of Jeremiah 29 (NKJV), a familiar passage in evangelical circles. Jeremiah sends a letter to the people of Judah as they are in the middle of a seventy-year exile. They are living in a city that is not their own, and have little hope of getting back to the safe bubble of Judah. The passage is most known for verse 11: "For I know the thoughts that I have towards you, says the Lord, thoughts of peace and not of evil, to give you a future and a hope." Or verse 13 "And you will seek me and find me when you search for me with all your heart."

But in that very same letter, Jeremiah wrote to the captives in verse 7, "Seek the peace and prosperity of the city to which I have carried you into exile. Pray to the Lord for it, because if it prospers, you too will prosper." Because business contributes to the peace and prosperity of a community, it should be a part of the total solution that we as Christians offer to the world. Even if we feel like we are in a foreign world, like the exiles who are receiving this letter from Jeremiah, God gives us opportunities through businesses to "seek the peace and prosperity of the city to which I have called you."

PERSONAL REFLECTION: Talented and committed Christians, and our voices, need to be present in every area of society —so we can provide flavor and influence the society and so we can provide opportunities for others.

The Apostle Paul wrote in 1 Corinthians 7:23 (NKJV), "You were bought at a price, do not become slaves of men." That verse can encourage us to avoid becoming a slave to our jobs, but I also hope we will not become slaves to the *idea* that the only meaningful way to live our lives is in full-time ministry.

How can you reflect to your colleagues at work the truth that God bought you at a price and that you belong to Him? How can you use the professional gifts He gave you for His purposes in your workplace?

CHAPTER 2

Where Does a Christian Woman Belong?
Recognizing women as image bearers of Christ

I recently had coffee with a young woman who is planning to enter the military. As she waits for acceptance into one of the branches of service, she is trying to get a job in the defense field. We didn't know much about each other; a woman we both knew from church simply introduced us. So we spent the first thirty minutes of our meeting chatting about where she could look for a job and people I knew with whom she could network. Then we started talking about life, and I mentioned that I had been working on this book.

Her response was immediate and strong, "Oh, my gosh, really? I can't wait to read it. No one ever talks about these things! I'm going to buy that book for all my friends."

Her affirmation was fabulous for me (she is an expressive young woman), but I got off of my ego trip and asked her why she was excited about this book and what about the topic interested her.

Her response was familiar to me: "I kept thinking if I was really serious about serving God, He'd call me to be a missionary. But I feel really drawn to go into the military." Then she told me that she was almost afraid to think about getting married and having children because, "I would feel like I'd have to stay at home and I'm not sure I'd want to do that full time."

As she continued, I heard these underlying questions: Am I less of a Christian woman if I choose to stay single, or if I choose to pursue a career? Am I allowed to have "authority" over men (whatever that means)? If I do get married, do I have to have children? And if I have children, what if I don't want to be at home full time?

Where the Questions Come from

We often developed our self-image from the important people and influences around us: if a parent, teacher, or coach saw gifts in us and encouraged us, those were likely the things we pursued. Similarly, if one of these people told us we weren't good at something, we may have decided not to pursue that interest or option.

As Christians, we need to understand that the church we attend, and the larger Church around us, has a huge influence on how we see ourselves. At church, either implicitly or explicitly, we sometimes hear the message, or even see examples, that enforce the perspective that (a) the "best" Christians go into full-time ministry, (b) women aren't supposed to lead men— ever, and (c) women should prioritize getting married over a career. If women do decide to get married, and if they decide to have children, the best way to prioritize their family is to be home full time.

As we prepare to talk more about the realities we face in our jobs, it's important to understand the challenges we may face even entering the professional world. It's important to have a good sense of our own theology about why we belong in the professional world, so we can better integrate our faith and our work.

I am fortunate to attend a church in which women's ministry is multi-dimensional, that recognizes the various roles women play in contemporary society. But I know it is not always that way, and professional women often feel excluded from traditional women's ministries. The stereotype of women gathering together for flowery, pink women's Bible studies that meet at 10:00 a.m. on Tuesday persists in our Christian culture. Those types of small groups—everything from their meeting times to the topics covered—send a message about what is expected of women.

Why don't we have many examples of strong professional women in our Christian circles? Why don't we feel encouraged in our vocational callings at church? I've spoken to many women who not only feel like they are lower on the hierarchy than full-time ministry workers or full-time moms, but they also feel like the church doesn't value their careers as much as it values men's careers. For example, when a man who is a plumber is asked to serve on the finance board of the church and a woman who is a CPA is asked to serve in children's ministry, it reflects a specific value system.

The young woman I enjoyed coffee with at the beginning of the chapter was communicating these explicit and implicit messages she's received at church over the years: that she should *want* to be a missionary, that she should plan to be a stay-at-home mom, and that she should avoid leadership opportunities if it looks like she'll be in charge "too much."

But as I said in the previous chapter, I don't believe all Christians should be in full-time ministry. Nor do I think much of the implication that all women should be homemakers. That is why the variety of ways that a woman can serve God is so important; if it is not addressed in church or if we receive mixed messages—i.e., that we can lead a co-ed missions trip, but we can't teach an adult, co-ed Sunday school class—confusion ensues. We then carry these confused perspectives about ourselves and the different roles we are allowed to fill into our professional worlds.

The Two Main Christian Perspectives

Put simply, our modern-day evangelical perspective on the role of, and place for, a woman is the result of Scripture and thousands of years of church history, tradition and interpretation. There are two generally accepted perspectives when it comes to discussing women's roles in the American, evangelical Christian subculture. This debate is where the Church gets its opinion (and sends out its prescriptions) for the types of roles and responsibilities women are allowed and encouraged to take on. Understanding these views can help us understand why we are even having this conversation. The first perspective is known as complementarian, which suggests that men and women are equal as persons and as human beings created in God's image, but there are gender distinctions when it comes to functional roles in the church and the home. The second view is known as egalitarian, which is the perspective that since we are all one in Christ, there are no gender distinctions. Women and men are equally qualified and called to serve in any position when it comes to functional roles in the church, and in the household.

As with most things that we try to simplify into two distinct categories, very few people fit neatly into one description or another. The range covers strong complementarians to strong egalitarians, moderates of each and subscribers of neither. As I describe the views here, I know that there is an array of perspectives in between and I do not intend to oversimplify but to give a general overview.

Strong complementarians interpret Bible verses like Titus 2:4-5[3] or 1 Timothy 2:11 and 2:12[4] as saying that women— married women—belong *almost exclusively* in the home, and should not be in a position of leading or teaching. It's from these verses that we get the idea that women should not be lead pastors and should not be able to have authority over men for religious instruction. Granted, in 1 Timothy, Paul is speaking specifically to a church, but people who hold this perspective sometimes apply it to other arenas as well, such as the workplace. Moderate complementarians say that Paul's instruction only applies to the church, limitations on women leading don't extend to the workplace.

Egalitarians look at these same verses and say that Paul was writing to Timothy about specific problems in specific churches

---

[3] Titus 2:4-5 "And so train the young women to love their husbands and children, to be self-controlled, pure, working at home, kind, and submissive to their own husbands, that the word of God may not be maligned."

[4] 1 Timothy 2:11-12 "Women should learn in silence with all subjection. I do not permit a woman to have authority over a man"

because Paul is referring to the religious instruction going on in Ephesus. At the time of this letter, Christian religious instruction was based on the Jewish model, which was not co-ed. When they tried mixing genders, the women continued to behave as they did in their women's classes where they led discussions, etc. Culturally, men weren't accustomed to learning from women at that time, and Paul thought Jesus' return was imminent, so there wasn't time to disturb cultural norms. But since we have co-ed instruction now, and men have acclimated to female teachers, egalitarians would say that Paul's specific instruction is not applicable to our culture.

Both groups also look to other verses to form their perspectives on the role of a woman. Genesis 1:28, for instance, points to the pre-fall relationship between Adam and Eve as that of equals, and egalitarians believe that if Christ came to restore the world to God's original design, then we should look at the example of that time *before* sin came into the world:

> *God blessed them and said to **them**, "Be fruitful and increase in number; fill the earth and subdue it. Rule over the fish in the sea and the birds in the sky and over every living creature that moves on the ground"* (Genesis 1:28, emphasis mine).

Complementarians emphasize the passage where God told Eve, after the fall, that her husband would rule over her (Genesis 4:16).

Egalitarians would move on to the Proverbs 31 woman, and her many celebrated characteristics, pointing specifically to her economic contributions: she buys a field and sells it, her trading is profitable, etc. She is participating in the economy and contributing to the support of her family. Complementarians view the same verses as an exhortation to "homemaking:" providing food for her household, etc.

Egalitarians draw another example from the account in John 4 when Jesus first revealed that He was the Son of God to the Samaritan woman at the well. And in Mark 16 and John 20 we see that Jesus chose to appear first to women when He was resurrected from the dead (Mark 16:9 and John 20:14). This was during a cultural period when a woman's word was not legally accepted as testimony in a court of law, and so egalitarians say Jesus was making a point when He selected these women.

Finally, the egalitarian perspective would point out the passage in Acts during Pentecost when the Spirit was poured out on men <u>and</u> women:

> *In the last days, God says,* **I will pour out my Spirit on all people. Your sons and daughters will prophesy,** *your young men will see visions, your old men will dream dreams.* **Even on my servants, both men and women, I will pour out my Spirit in those days, and they will prophesy** (Acts 2:17-18 NIV, emphasis mine).

Complementarians cite the absence of women among the disciples and original church leaders as an indicator of the natural structure for male/female relationships within the church, and they apply that interpretation to society as a whole.

Complementarians would say that while these structures may not fully use the gifting of some women, God desires an order in the church, Scripture tells us that order and those who believe otherwise are defying Biblical authority.

Egalitarians say that while Paul was writing within the social conventions of the time, Christ came to turn those conventions on their heads. And He drove that point home by allowing women to accompany Him in His ministry and relying on their financial support (Luke 8:1-3).

Complementarians emphasize that Jesus' statement about the bride of Christ in Ephesians 5:25-27 signifies Him as the husband and the leader, and the Church represents the wife, who submits to her husband's leadership. Egalitarians lean on the relationship within the Trinity—where all parts are equal and enjoy shared roles.

So Which Am I?

The questions surrounding a woman's role/place/potential for leadership in the Church have been argued for centuries. I'm not a Greek or Hebrew scholar, and I agree that careful exegesis—that is, critical explanation or interpretation of text—is required to gain full understanding of these passages. Please know that I don't take these issues lightly and believe that any time we interpret Scripture and advise people how to apply it to their lives, we walk on holy ground.

I have wrestled with these two perspectives in my own life, especially as I contemplated this book in general and researched this chapter in particular. I asked the same questions many other professional Christian women have asked: What does Scripture really say? How should cultural context—both the time during which Scripture was written and the cultural context of when we are reading it—be taken into consideration? Are Paul's letters more important than the Garden of Eden or the illustrations of Deborah, Proverbs 31, Esther, Junia, or Priscilla? Is the one *doctrine* telling us how women should be while the other is a *narrative* that paints pictures of healthy women leaders across cultural struggles at any given time, but perhaps doesn't "count" as much as doctrine?

Put another way, what *do* I believe Scripture says, even if my culture says Scripture is wrong? Which culture influences me more when reading Scripture—21st-century Western culture, or 21st-century evangelical culture?

A lot of our conversations about women's roles stop on this binary teeter-totter, discussing which perspective is correct, as if there are only two perspectives. Many times in my head I've repeated the Rupertus Meldenius quote (that is often misattributed to Saint Augustine): *"In the essentials, unity; in the non-essentials, liberty; in all things, charity."* I used to wonder how critical this disagreement about gender roles was: *is* it an "essential" and should there be unity? Is it a "non-essential" in which there should be liberty? Or is it enough simply to acknowledge that there should be charity—even if it's hard— when one group of people thinks it's an essential and another group thinks it's a non-essential?

I'm still working through this issue myself but here's why I think it's important to us as working women: I believe God has given every *person* gifts, skills, opportunities and callings. Each *person* should have the opportunity to flourish to the fullest extent of his or her giftings regardless of age, socioeconomic status, geography or gender.

When we believe that there are only a few ways for a woman to express her gifts and abilities, we shut off a whole range of possibilities for God to express His creativity and variety. As the theologian Oswald Chambers said, "Never make a principle out of your experience. Allow God to be as original with other people as He is with you."

So for those of us who are in the workplace because God gave us unique gifts, we are to use those gifts to the best and fullest of our abilities is to honor Him, not to dishonor Him. But when the Church doesn't show us that value, or it doesn't recognize it when we're begging to contribute what we've been given, namely our unique talents and gifts, we are failing to fully utilize "half the church."

Author Carolyn Custis James drives this point home, along with highlighting many of the tragic implications, in her recent book, *Half the Church:*

> Are God's purposes for women only for those whose lives go from early adulthood to "I do" and from there to the delivery room? Or are His purposes dynamic enough to leave no woman or girl behind? But it wasn't until Half the Sky[5] took me to the forgotten fringes of female existence that I began to grasp how far this commitment was leading and that even those questions were too narrow. What if a

---

[5] "Half the Sky" is a book calling for solutions to empower women and girls, by Nicholas Kristof and Sheryl DuWunn.

soul is completely ravaged—brutalized and dehumanized until there is nothing left but an empty shell? Does the gospel only offer such a woman salvation or does it also establish her as a participant in the Grand Story that God is weaving in the world? Are God's purposes for his daughters indestructible, or do they collapse under the weight of the world's evils?[6]

When we deny women the opportunity to use their gifts, it leads to devaluation and oppression. It's one thing to encounter that perspective in the Western evangelical church where it means that we don't have the opportunity to teach on Sunday mornings, or that some women feel trapped in their suburban lifestyles. It's another thing altogether to encounter that perspective in other parts of the world where the devaluing of women translates into deep abuses, human trafficking, and overall degradation. But both of these environments—from the lack of women in leadership in the West to the severe oppression of women in other parts of the world—stem from the same root problem: not recognizing women as image bearers of Christ, and not recognizing that the Holy Spirit doesn't discriminate based on a person's gender. I don't believe we should rest our understanding of women on anything other than Jesus' view and value of them.

In other words, I no longer think this is a "non-essential." After many long and thoughtful discussions and much reading, I see this in fact as an integral aspect toward being who God

---

[6] Custis James, Carolyn, *Half the Church*, Zondervan 2010, pg 35.

made us to be. One book in particular, *How I Changed My Mind on Women in Leadership*, a compilation of essays from today's evangelical leaders, exposed just how important this issue is. In the foreword, Dallas Willard writes, "The issue of women in leadership is not a minor or marginal one. It profoundly affects the sense of identity and worth on *both* sides of the gender line; and, if wrongly grasped, it restricts the resources for blessing, through the church, upon an appallingly needy world."[7]

So, What Should We Do?

I believe the Church should be on the forefront of helping women realize the fullness of their potential—in any role. When the Church only has women in support roles, mainly related to family or children's ministry, it makes me question this calling I feel on my life from God to be in the business world. Much like the young woman I met with in the cafe, I wonder sometimes if I'm doing something wrong. But I shouldn't feel this way if I'm responding to God's call on my life. Consequently, I feel a personal responsibility to help the Church send a clear message to women who feel a vocational calling on their lives. I want to encourage them to support what professional women are doing, and to provide role models who demonstrate what it means to contribute in all spheres of life. We desperately need more realistic representations of women in churches.

In June of 2006, writer/director Joss Whedon (*Firefly, Buffy the Vampire Slayer, Serenity, The Avengers*) received an award

---

[7] Johnson, Alan F. *How I Changed My Mind about Women in Leadership.* 2010. Zondervan, Grand Rapids, Michigan.

from Equality Now, a non-profit organization that is dedicated to achieving legal and systemic change that addresses violence and discrimination against women and girls around the world. The evening he received the award was a celebration "honoring men on the front lines" in the fight for women's equality.[8]

While accepting the award, he explained that he'd been part of many press junkets where he was continually asked the same questions about why he creates such strong female characters in his shows and movies. He said, "When you're asked something 500 times, you really start to think about the answer." In the course of his acceptance speech, he role-played as a reporter and himself. Here are some of his answers:

> *Joss playing a reporter*: "So, Joss, I would like to know, why do you always write these strong women characters?"
> Whedon: "I think it's because of my mother. She really was an extraordinary, inspirational, tough, cool, sexy, funny woman and that's the kind of woman I've always surrounded myself with."

> *Playing another reporter*: "Why do you write these strong women characters?"
> Whedon: "My father and my stepfather had a lot to do with it, because they prized wit and resolve in the women they were with above all things. And they were among the rare men who

---

[8] Whedon, Joss. Equality Now Acceptance Speech. June 2006

understood that recognizing somebody else's power does not diminish your own. When I created Buffy, I wanted to create a female icon, but I also wanted to be very careful to surround her with men who not only had no problem with the idea of a female leader, but, were in fact, engaged and even attracted to the idea."

Playing another reporter: "So, why do you create these strong, how you say, the women—(I'm in Europe now, so, it's very, it's international)—these strong women characters?"
Whedon: "Well, because these stories give people strength, and I've heard it from a number of people, and I've felt it myself, and it's not just women, it's men, and I think there is something particular about a female protagonist that allows a man to identify with her that opens up something, that he might—an aspect of himself—that he might be unable to express—hopes and desires—he might be uncomfortable expressing through a male identification figure."

Yet another reporter: "So, why do you create these strong women characters?"
Whedon: "Cause they're hot."

The Umpteenth Reporter: But, these strong women characters…

Whedon: "Why are you even asking me this?! How is it possible that this is even a question? Honestly, seriously, why did you write that down? Why aren't you asking a hundred other guys why they don't write strong women characters? I believe that what I am doing should not be remarked upon, let alone honored and there are other people doing it. But, seriously, this question is ridiculous and you just gotta stop."

He continues: "Equality is not a concept. It's not something we should be striving for. It's a necessity. Equality is like gravity; we need it to stand on this earth as men and women. And the misogyny that is in every culture is life out of balance and that imbalance is sucking something out of the soul of every man and woman who is confronted with it. We need equality. Kind-of now."

The way women are portrayed in entertainment shapes how everyone—both men and women—perceive women. Likewise, how women are portrayed in the Church shapes how we see ourselves, and how men see us. When we see people who look like us at church (same gender, same age, same race) what roles are they filling? What does it tell us about our own abilities? Our own potential? Does it show us the range of things we could pursue? Or does it restrict our vision for ourselves and other women?

The Church, perhaps more than the entertainment industry, should be on the forefront of helping people understand the value of women and the tremendous resources they provide to address the world's overwhelming problems. We should be standing up next to Joss Whedon banging on a podium for the end to this question, "Where do Christian women belong?" But until there's no longer a need for that question, churches should be talking about it, and they should be holding up women from all spheres of life as examples of Godly women —not just those who choose to have children and stay home full time, or those who volunteer with the children's ministry. Those are valuable callings in life, but not the only callings for women.

Getting Back to Work

I think there still exists a lingering perception—among men AND women—that women aren't equal to men in church and that they aren't as capable as men to lead, make complicated decisions, or "get things done." Knowingly or unknowingly, we've carried this perception over to our professional environment. I recognize that this isn't a problem exclusive to the evangelical gender dynamic. But for now, let's talk about the Church. Without untangling how the perspectives we gain in church influence us—and how those perspectives may be inaccurate—it's no small thing trying to figure out where we belong professionally or the types of roles we can undertake. In fact, it can feel muddled. If we hear that our contribution is to be determined in relation to the closest man, we carry that perspective with us everywhere we go—to work, into dating relationships, into our hobbies or volunteer activities. If we hear that a woman's place is in the home or that she shouldn't lead, we are hesitant to excel or pursue opportunities at our jobs.

Mutual Respect

How we choose to live out God's calling on our lives is where it gets interesting, and I do mean interesting in the best sense of the word: unique, varied, colorful, beautiful—interesting. Some of my friends have chosen lives as full-time homemakers, and I love when they love what they do. Some of my friends have chosen to work as full-time advocates for the poor and broken among us, and I love when they love what they do. Others of my friends choose lives as artists, making beautiful, complicated pieces that communicate the diversity of God, and I love when they love what they do. We all may find different opportunities in different seasons of life, but I think we should celebrate any woman living out fully the gifts that God has given her.

As a church, we need to recognize that we have been involved in perpetuating the ideas that women's gifts only extend so far. True, some parts of the Church in the U.S. are changing—sometimes explicitly, sometimes in more subtle ways—but we can't ignore that there are centuries of prejudices to overcome. And we can't ignore that these prejudices have much more dire consequences in other parts of the world.

While I pointed out at the beginning of this chapter that we often get our self-image from our parents, our friends, our spouses, our culture, and our church, our self-image must be rooted in God's view of us. Who *He* tells us we are is the most important perspective we can have on ourselves. Rather than forcing ourselves into roles based solely on our gender, we should use our natural, God-given, talents, wherever they may take us. If we can respect how God calls us each uniquely, and that our calling may not look like our neighbors, we'll go a long way toward becoming women who are fully engaged in God's work. The bottom line: it's not about gender, we are all His image bearers.

PERSONAL REFLECTION: Consider some of the roles where women in your church often serve. What do those roles communicate about women? Do you feel free to contribute your gifts and talents?

Spend some time praying for your community, that a corporate vision as God's image-bearers would transcend gender.

CHAPTER 3

Finding Our Work/Life Balance

I used to cringe whenever I heard the phrase, "work/life balance." I would immediately assume the implication was that work was bad because there was "too much work and not enough life." As if there was a work/life version of "Lady Justice" whose scale held one tray of work and one tray of life and the two were always lopsided and never met.

Then I began wondering which activities in my life belonged in which category. Did meeting my colleagues for dinner qualify as work? Did going to the gym on my lunch hour fit in my "life" category? Or were these activities interconnected, part of a whole that made for a more meaningful lifestyle?

The tension led me to more questions: If we believe that there isn't a secular/sacred divide, and if our job is what God is calling us to, what, then, qualifies as work? And, what qualifies as life? Certainly, we wouldn't expect a pastor to restrict his or her work to a 40-hour workweek, neatly contained between 9-and-5, Mondays through Fridays.

Regardless of whether we are a full-time women's ministry leader, a full-time mother, or a full-time junior analyst, I am not recommending we run ourselves into the ground, doing nothing but our "jobs." Obviously, there are times when I've worked late nights and weekends on projects that seemed to have no end in sight, leaving little time for sleep, exercise, friends, or "spiritual pursuits." And I don't recommend that as a permanent way of life.

But I do think we've taken cultural expectations of a workweek and made them rigid spiritual expectations. Where I live in Washington, D.C., I often take the Metro (our subway system). One day I noticed graffiti next to the Red Line that said, *"The 40-hour workweek, brought to you by America's Labor Union."* Our current concept of the workweek (what I meant by cultural expectations) came about during the Industrial Revolution, and I'm certainly glad that there are regulations that are supposed to keep companies from working people into the ground. Still, the point of a job is not merely to punch a time clock and earn a paycheck. In fact, when we understand that our work might actually be a calling from God instead of just a way to pay our bills we also begin to realize that there is another way to achieve a work/life blend.

Seasons of Life

Where we are at the moment—both personally and professionally—greatly influences our work/life balance. A twenty-something fresh out of college may have more freedom in her schedule than a forty-something who has three children in grade school. The twenty-something can choose to use that freedom to attend Bible studies and church activities, or to work longer hours, get involved in recreational activities, or whatever she finds interesting. The forty-something's choice to have children, on the other hand, greatly influences her priorities and schedule. A single mother in her 40s with three children may not have the option of working only one job for forty hours a week; providing for her children may demand much more than that. In other words, our present season of life will influence how we balance our work with our other life-options.

Professional opportunities and interests influence our work/life balance as well. I knew a woman, a mother of two, who had been a waitress in diners for years and wanted to open her own restaurant. She and her husband made major time commitments to make that dream come true—they both worked longer hours in their day jobs and spent evenings and weekends getting their restaurant ready. The first several years were tough and they experienced trial, error, redirection and long, long hours. After those initial years, her schedule calmed down considerably, but even now she certainly doesn't work traditional hours.

Another woman I know was dedicated to public service and spent months working on Barack Obama's first presidential campaign. After he won the election, she received a Presidential appointment to his administration and worked far more than forty hours a week, almost every week of the year. She had the opportunity to do something that was important to her, where she believed she was making a difference, and even when she wasn't officially 'on the clock', she chose to spend more of her time in her job.

On a different part of the spectrum, I have another friend who, along with her husband, decided to find jobs that allowed them both to work only 32-hours per week. They made financial adjustments to accommodate less than full-time paychecks, and told me how grateful they are for the extra time they get to spend together while also pursuing other interests.

The point is that balancing our life with our work can't be reduced to one specific formula that works for every woman. God-sized dreams about what we want to do with our lives don't always come in 40-hour-a-week packages.

None of these examples advocates a workaholic lifestyle, nor do they support the position that one arrangement is better than another. Instead, they demonstrate that during different seasons in our lives, we need to make different choices as we respond to God's call, knowing that our work/life balance will evolve over the course of our lives.

Big Rocks

Navigating the seasons of our lives requires we also understand what our priorities are. A sermon illustration I've always enjoyed might help demonstrate this: imagine a pastor standing at the front of a church with a large pickle jar. He begins putting fist-sized rocks in the jar until no more will fit. He asks the congregation, "Is the jar full?" and they reply, "Yes." But then he pulls out a container of pebbles, pours them into the pickle jar, and they fill in around the big rocks. He asks everyone, "Now, is it full?" and people respond, "Yes." Next, he brings out a bag of sand and pours it in so it fills in around the pebbles. This time, people have caught on and answer, "No," when he asks if the jar is full. He completes the illustration with a pitcher of water that soaks into the sand. He asks, "What is the lesson here?"

"You can always fit more in," replies someone from the congregation.

"No. The point is that you have to put the big rocks in first," the pastor responds.

If we were to fill our schedule with "water" and then tried to put in pebbles or even big rocks, the contents of our jars would spill over. We have to know what the most important things are in our lives, in priority order, and then build our schedules accordingly.

We need to prioritize, because realistically we can't always fit more in. That's no small thing though, considering the type of world we live in, one where we are always trying to squeeze more in, and then are surprised when we're exhausted and overwhelmed. The Bible is clear about some priorities. Matthew 6:33 tells us that our first priority should be our relationship with God: "Seek *first* the Kingdom of God and His righteousness, and all these things will be added unto you." In Colossians 3:23 we are called to work honorably and well: "Whatever you do, work at it with all your heart, as though you are working for the Lord and not for man." Each of us must determine how much time we need to spend developing our relationship with God, how much time we need to dedicate to our families, and then continue down the list of our priorities.

But while Scripture sets up the parameters, God doesn't dictate what life looks like down to the hour for each of us. That's why we need to determine which are our big rocks (within the parameters of Scripture), which are our pebbles, and which are our sand and water. Some people I know sit down and explicitly list the number of hours they would dedicate to each pursuit, and factor out how much they'll have left over for the next priority. We can "attack hours," or we can try to determine the type of life we want to live setting our priorities to fit our desired lifestyle.

Getting Our Priorities Straight

This idea of priorities is essential for career-oriented women, and requires we demonstrate spiritual maturity when making choices about how to spend our time. God is our ultimate "boss" whether we work inside or outside the home. We must seek to bring Him honor and glory with our priorities and decisions. Honoring God first will ultimately bring honor to our families as well.

In the past year, my husband Andy and I both have taken on some pretty big personal projects—for me, it was this book. Both of our endeavors take a lot of time and energy. We've had numerous conversations about how to do these projects with excellence, and how to make sure our other priorities are in line. During one of those conversations, Andy turned to me and said, "We've agreed our priorities are, in this order: God, each other, our family and close friends, our callings, friends and neighbors. We are each free to chase dreams and pursue opportunities in the context of these priorities."

His commitment to working with me in prioritizing our lives means that he loves the idea of me writing a book, and the opportunities that go with it, in so far as it doesn't crowd out God, him, and our family and close friends.

There may be a time that I have to choose between a conference and a weekend with him, and I may choose the conference. Because my calling is important to both of us, he understands that. But it's not as important as our marriage, and so this book should not be regularly trumping all the other priorities on the list.

I'm not someone who thinks I can "have it all," especially not "at the same time." Life takes time. Doing things well— things like having relationships (with God, family, friends), doing our job well, raising children, pursuing personal projects, working for a cause we believe in—all of them take time. And all of them force us to answer the tough question: *which things are most important to us?*

Was Jesus Balanced?

And determining which values are most important takes us back to the One who calls us to Himself: Jesus. I've read arguments about whether Jesus Himself was balanced. Some people point to the first chapter of Mark's gospel—which documents the early days of Jesus' ministry—to argue that He always accommodated those who bombarded Him with needs. Others point out that He always made prayer and rest a priority.

Either way, one of the most important work/life balance lessons to take from Jesus' lifestyle, is that, whether in work or in rest, He always obeyed the Father. Whether He removed Himself from the crowds to go to the garden to pray, or performed miracles for individuals in front of the masses or the disciples, Jesus *obeyed* God. In John 5:30, Jesus says, "By myself I can do nothing; I judge only as I hear, and my judgment is just, for I seek not to please myself but Him who sent me," (NIV).

When seeking to prioritize our lives by finding a work/ life balance, this lesson of obedience to God is one we need to adopt. We often believe that "balance" will solve our problems. But life keeps happening and we continually find ourselves saying, if we can just get through this next hectic time at work, soccer season for the kids, this relative's illness, etc., then we'll have more balance, more rest, and everything will be better.

I can't tell you how many women I've heard say, "It's just a really busy season right now." Really? How many times does basketball season start right after soccer? Every year. When one busy season at work ends, often another busy season begins. When one family crisis resolves itself, often a friend needs our help. But if we have set our priorities by obeying the Father, by letting Him dictate our "big rocks," that is where we will find the right life for us. Jesus, Himself, is our balance.

The Sabbath Rest

Whether or not Jesus was "perfectly balanced" by current standards doesn't matter. What does matter is that He understood how times of rest and renewal allowed Him to live the full life to which God had called Him. While we may not be "under the law" to strictly observe the Sabbath, the concept is important. It directs us to find ways to incorporate rest—regardless of the season of life.

It's harder and harder to find times of rest in our 24/7 world. Yet, however we choose to rest, we cannot underestimate its importance for our corporate and individual lives. Sabbath is a time we need to set-apart as holy, to remind us of Him who makes us holy, and to remind us that we are to be holy. It is a time to be refreshed and refined, and not enough of us make time for it.

The Sabbath historically has been about taking breaks from what we usually do for work. In biblical times, a lot of the work was manual, and rest meant taking a break from difficult physical labor so that bodies could be restored. God mandated a Sabbath rest both for restoration and for remembering those priorities He set. Even God rested after the six days of creation!

Today, many of us perform primarily mental work at our jobs, so it's not uncommon to find we're "active rest-ers" by the time weekends roll around. We can observe the Sabbath principle by shutting down from our [mainly mental] work through getting outside and enjoying God's creation, hiking or gardening or bicycling. Even walking the dog. By engaging our bodies actively, we often give our minds a chance to be quiet.

It's not like Christians are the only people who know the importance of rest. Research shows that taking a break actually increases your performance level—allowing you to refocus, to tackle problems with improved energy. You only have to look to the growing popularity of yoga (20.4 million Americans in 2012, according to *Yoga Journal*), or the push for more vacation time to see that people desire time to recharge.

As Christians though, God has given us permission to rest as we observe the Sabbath—something our jobs, families and other commitments don't often give us the space to do. We don't *have* to observe the Sabbath or be intentional in a day of rest. We *get* to observe the Sabbath! We can—and should—

look forward to it! In her book *Keeping the Sabbath Wholly*, theologian Marva Dawn provides an inspiring framework to cease (cease work, anxiety, trying to be God), rest (physical, spiritual, social rest), embrace (embrace intentionality, time, wholeness), and feast (feast on beauty, music, food).[9] She stresses that the Sabbath should be seen as a celebration and observing it actually enables us to approach the rest of our lives with more focus and renewed attention.

For me, Sundays used to be a day full of church activities —pre-church prayer, church services, post-church homeless ministry, lunch with church friends, football with church friends. While those activities are valuable, eventually they ceased to be restful for me and I'd find myself worn out on Sunday nights. And, to be honest, so many church activities ironically weren't very worshipful either.

After we got married, my husband and I rediscovered going to church on Saturday nights. Now we enjoy worshiping with our church mainly on Saturday nights, and then we try to spend Sundays "working" in our garden, or meeting friends for a picnic or going for a hike (try being the operative word, sometimes we have to work, or do chores). We've come to see Sabbath rest as something that helps us unplug from our regular world, expressing our thanks to God for providing for our needs, including rest. Rest—we've come to learn—has become an essential component to balancing our work with our shared life, helping us remember the priorities we've set in the light of God's grace and call during this season of life.

---

9 Dawn, Marva. *Keeping the Sabbath Wholly.* Wm. B. Eerdmans Publishing Company

PERSONAL REFLECTION: Perspectives on work/life balance in the Christian community take many different forms. Perhaps in this chapter you were expecting: "Three easy steps to finding better work/life balance," And now you're slightly disappointed to discover there's no such formula. But I do hope it has caused you to think about what "work" is for you, and what "life" means to you. I also hope that you'll take some time to figure out what your "big rocks" are, and just how big they are.

How can you give those "rocks" the time they need, and create space for life-giving worship of God and spiritual renewal? How can you integrate the parts of your life, the sleeping and waking hours, your time with your family and your job, to see them not as separate entities that need to be kept apart, but as important parts of a whole life?

What does your priority list look like? What is on it? What is the order of the items? Ask God to guide you each day as you rest in Him and the work He's doing in your life.

CHAPTER 4

Determining Our Calling

A lot of us would say we understand God's *general* calling for His people. We are all called, for instance, to a relationship with Him, knowing that *We love God because He first loved us,* (1John 4:19). We are all called to love Him and to love others, as Luke writes in 10:27, the greatest commandment: *Love the Lord your God with all your heart and with all your soul and with all your strength and with all your mind; and, Love your neighbor as yourself.* And we are all called to take care of widows and orphans, and to keep ourselves free from the world's evil influence, beautifully describesd in James 1:27 (NCV): *Religion that God the Father accepts as pure and without fault is this: caring for orphans or widows who need help, and keeping yourself free from the world's evil influence.*

But when we discuss our unique "callings," we are most often referring to that special assignment from God—what you and only you were designed to do. If only we knew what that was.

We tend to think of our calling mostly in terms of our occupation. But Heather Zempel, the discipleship pastor at National Community Church in Washington, D.C., cautions people against thinking their calling is only about a specific task:

> When you think about the call of God, do you understand that to be a call to what you do, a call to where you are, a call to who you are with, or a call to who you are becoming? Sometimes, God calls us to a specific place: Abraham was called to a land that he would be shown. Other times, God calls us to specific people: Paul was called to the Gentiles. His location changed and his task changed—sometimes he was a tent-maker, sometimes he was an itinerant preacher—but he was always called to the Gentiles. Most importantly, God's calling for all of us involves the person we are becoming. I am learning more and more that God is more interested in the person we are becoming than in the work we are doing.[10]

Opening the aperture of what we consider to be our calling gives us more space—and less angst—about determining a discrete answer. But I believe that happens only when we hone in on something Zempel said in the middle of the paragraph, "God's calling for all of us involves the person we are becoming."

[10] *Kaleidoscope Calling.* Heather Zempel. January 11, 2011.

Our calling isn't only a job, any more than we might be called to a people group, or a place. No, our calling rather includes *our whole being*. It's to be the person God created us to be, and we live that calling out *in* our jobs, or *with* specific people, or in a particular place. And most importantly—our calling is always to Him.

How to Determine Our Calling

Regardless of whether our calling is to a specific job, a people group, a place, or whether it's a call to become "who we were born to be," we all want to know how to determine what *it* is. And most of us would prefer to discover *it* in three easy steps, just like finding balance. Don't we wish!

In his book *Wishful Thinking*, author Frederick Buechner offers the simplest yet most profound definition of calling I've come across yet: "The place God calls you to is where your deep gladness and the world's deep hunger meet." [11]

Sometimes we think of our calling as responding to the "world's deepest hunger," but too often we forget about "our deep gladness." I've heard Christians say, "This is the hardest thing I could do, so it must be what God is calling me to." But this way of thinking misses something.

Do I think our callings will be tough? Sometimes. Do I think the only point of our lives is our own happiness or gladness? Of course not—I believe we are first and foremost called to be holy. Do I believe that holiness is sometimes formed through great trial? Yes. But do I think God only calls us to the difficult? No. I think God often uses the difficult journey to reveal His holy

---

[11] Buechner, Frederick; *Wishful Thinking: A Theological ABC.* 1973. page 95

purposes to us, but I don't believe that means we should seek out the most uncomfortable situations we can find to try to create our own sanctification. God has wired us with gifts and preferences—our deep gladness—and that can be a substantial part of our calling.

So how do we figure out what constitutes our deep gladness? Kent Julian, a Christian life and career coach in Atlanta, Georgia, helps people discern their callings. The process he employs starts with a question modeled after a movie reference. In the movie "City Slickers," a protagonist has the following exchange with an old cowboy:

Curly: Do you know what the secret of life is?
[*holds up one finger*]
Curly: This.
Mitch: Your finger?
Curly: One thing. Just one thing. You stick to that and the rest don't mean sh*t.
Mitch: But, what is the 'one thing?'
Curly: [*smiles*] That's what *you* have to find out.

Julian asks people he's working with what the *one thing* is that, if they boil everything else down, brings meaning, purpose, and significance to their lives. As believers, we are almost conditioned to answer that question with, "Christ." But Julian says it's incomplete to stop there and so he goes a step further: What is it about Christ that speaks to our souls?

Julian then follows up with two more questions: How does that *one thing* influence us at the core of our being, and how does that *one thing* affect what we do? In other words, considering probing questions like these helps us identify what

56

gives our lives meaning, discern how each affects us as people, and descide what we should do with that knowledge. We look at the passions God has given us, the specific character traits he has given us to live out, and then we set out to engage in activities that allow us to use those character traits.

My friend Rebecca says that finding our calling is a "combination of knowing God and knowing how God created you." We must first seek to know God, and as we do, we come to know ourselves.

Knowing ourselves, though, can be a tricky thing; it can be a fun and sometimes hard, revealing process that can be well worth the effort. As we come to know God more intimately through Scripture and through His body, we begin to see ourselves more clearly. But there are also other tools available for getting to know ourselves better, including Birkman Assessments or the Meyers-Briggs test. Taken in the light of God's grace, these tools help us develop a better idea of who we are, allowing us to articulate what we do and don't like. And the classic resource, *What Color is Your Parachute?*, is also great for identifying what kind of job we might fit well with, which could assist us in determining our vocational callings.

Whatever resources we use, with Scripture as our anchor, we need to learn to identify our unique gifting and preferences, both of which further reflect our identity in Christ. As we do, we start to see how that "one thing" can be applied to many different pursuits.

Spoiled for Choice

Not long ago in this country, it was expected that if a

young person had the opportunity to finish either high school or college, he or she would then "settle down" with a job and a family—likely the same job their parents had, in the same location as their parents had raised them. But when the industrial revolution began to create more choices for us, other life options arose. Now, in a knowledge-based economy, we have freedom of movement and freedom of job opportunities like no one has ever seen before. The result? It's not uncommon to hear of people spending their twenties to "figure themselves out."

The current academic term is "emerging adulthood," coined in part by Clark University psychologist Jeffrey Arnett Jensen. Jensen describes this phase as a time of transition, of "identity exploration, instability, self-focus, feeling in-between and . . . a sense of possibilities."

For those of us who fit in—or near—this category, we find an amazing amount of possibilities available to us, and even more so for women as professional options increase. And yet, with all these choices, it becomes more and more difficult to know just *what* we want to do—or should do.

This vocational angst that we see in many of today's twenty-somethings is complex and somewhat disconcerting. (And I say this as someone who has carried some of that angst into my thirties.) We literally have the whole world before us, but we are often so overwhelmed with the myriad opportunities, that we can rarely settle into one particular place, let alone one career. It's a little like surfing the Internet, spending time on one site only to grow bored quickly and click to another, more glitzy site. As we do, the illusion of 'bigger or better' often distracts us from the authentic roles God has for us.

So how do we know the specific area to which God is calling us? With so many unique positions, jobs that didn't even exist when our parents were young, how do we discern what our professional calling is?

Once again, there is no easy formula. Now, when it comes to picking a job in the land of opportunity, we are "spoiled for choice." Renata Salecl, a Slovenian philosopher, wrote in her book *Choice*, "the simplistic search for the perfect choice is not only impractical, but leads to misery."[12] Her point is that because we have so many options, we keep looking for "perfect," which we will never find. And that leads to disappointment.

This, of course, is true for many areas of our life, whether we are looking for a job, a spouse, a church, you name it. We have so many options now for so many things, but none of them are perfect matches. And the more we keep looking for them, the more likely we will only discover disillusionment.

Often when I speak with other Christians who are also professionals, there is a lot of talk about "your calling," as though there is one, and only one, option for how to spend our life in a way that is meaningful. For example, in a Bible study I led recently for professional women in Washington, prayer requests often included "finding my calling." One woman in the middle of her job search—I'll call her Rachel—had received two offers. What if she chose the wrong one? How could she know the true will of God? And would she ruin her life if she chose the wrong path? Rachel felt so much pressure to get her vocational calling "right" that she became paralyzed by the possibility of making a mistake.

---

[12] Saleci, Renata; *Choice*. Profile Publishers, 2010.

Another woman in our Bible study noted that Rachel's anxiety reminded her of the passage in the book of Hebrews comparing spiritual "infant food" to "solid food" for adults. Hebrews 5 explores the characteristics of leaders within the church, and one of the characteristics required is maturity and discernment. Hebrews 5:14 says, "But solid food is for the mature, who because of practice, have their senses trained to discern good and evil," (NASB).

This woman related the verse to a child's nutritional choices. At first, our parents put vegetables on our plate. We have no choice but to eat them. Then, a few years later, our parents ask us if we want peas or carrots with dinner, effectively limiting our choices but giving us some room to use the discernment we gained about vegetables as young children. As we grew, however, our parents trusted our ability to make wise decisions based on a more informed understanding of nutritional principles.

It's the same with God, she said to us: as we mature and move from eating infant food to solid spiritual food, our relationship with God matures. At this point our faith enables us to make the right decisions—because through practice, we have learned to discern good and evil. Our faith in God should never paralyze us with fear so that we don't know exactly what to do.

Put another way, we can see the "will of God" as a wide road with clear barriers on either side. But within the broad road, we can take many paths in accordance with God's will. This is not to imply that God will never speak to us specifically about one career choice over another, but as we mature it is important to trust the character God has been developing *in* us and realize that if we're living the *life* God called us to—our holistic calling, our whole person—then we can choose one of many professional callings and be fruitful and productive. We don't need to resign ourselves to chasing the one, perfect professional calling that, truthfully, may never materialize. As Saint Augustine said, "Love God and do what you want." The more we love Him, the more His character is formed in us and our decision-making is sound because we have the Mind of Christ. The goal is that our "wants" are shaped by His presence in our life.

I often have to remind other women (and myself) that the first and most important step towards discernment is to pray and listen for God's leading *before* asking our girlfriends, colleagues or other mentors. Ultimately it is God whom we serve in these settings. While he may not give an immediately clear response, I believe Scripture has much to say that encourages us to remain open to the doors He opens and the opportunities He puts in front of us.

Does Our Calling Change?

The older I get, the more I believe this question of whether our calling changes is the wrong question. The better question is how do *we* as Christ's followers keep changing and growing regardless of where God has placed us in our respective careers?

Kent Julian noted it's not so much that our calling changes, but that we learn to live it out better. "It's more that *you* change," he said. "Your *work* isn't your calling, what you do isn't your calling." Instead, Julian believes that how we fulfill our life's mission statement is what matters most when we think about calling. "I don't believe work is my calling," he continued, "work is what allows me to live out my calling,"

People seem to get more clarity on their vocational callings, and especially their overall callings, as they progress through life. I was listening to Dave Buehring (leader of Lionshare Discipleship Group) once talk about people who "hit their stride." He said it's often not until people are in their mid-fifties that they see all their prior work and experiences come together.

I have to admit, when I heard him say that, I felt a bit deflated. Not that I want to "peak" in my thirties and head downhill from there, but what he meant for encouragement initially made me feel like I have years before I'll do anything of value. However, that's not what he was trying to communicate. He went on to reassure those of us in the room that all of our experiences have value, but he didn't want those of us in our twenties, thirties or forties to be discouraged if we felt like we hadn't quite figured it all out. As we have more experiences that allow us to hone our skills and try new roles, we come to understand ourselves better. We've had more time to get to know God's character, and we become confident in where the road's twists and turns have taken us.

In the last few years, a good friend has changed professions and endured a period of unemployment. She said she still felt it was the will of God when she was unemployed, because she knew she was living out the calling of *who* she was supposed to be, that her calling wasn't dependent on a particular occupation. That time between jobs even came with some unexpected benefits: she was more present to focus on her young marriage and she was available to address several family emergencies that occurred. In this way she was obeying the holistic calling on her life, while her vocational calling was out of focus. While the period presented some confusion and frustration, she also had the perspective to see that time as a gift.

What Your Calling is *Not*

Regardless of how our professional work might change throughout our lives, we need to remember that there are also several things our calling is *not*. The first is that our calling is *not* instant. The Bible is full of accounts of people who had to wait for their callings, or wait for their callings to become reality. Sarai, the wife of Abram, was approximately 65 years old when God promised her and Abram a child and told Abram he was to be the "father of nations." But Sarai didn't have that baby until she was about 90 years old! God's timing required another 25 years of waiting, after she'd already lived a long life.

Moses was a shepherd while waiting on God's call for 40 years, and was already 80 years old when God appeared to him at the burning bush. Joseph believed God called him to something great, but spent seven years as a slave, and then another seven years as a prisoner, before he had the opportunity to start to live out His calling. We need to learn to be patient when issues with our jobs or expectations don't line up exactly the way we thought they should.

Our calling is also *not* risk-free. My husband is an active guy who loves to try new things. As a result, he's had more than his fair share of accidents. A few years ago he was playing football and broke his arm. He asked the doctor who was setting the break, if he was doing something wrong: Was he reckless? Did he have weak bones?

The doctor looked at him seriously and said, "Actually, the British have a cure for broken bones. They call it *tea*." He then elaborated, "If you don't want to break any more bones, sit down and drink tea every afternoon. But I suggest you keep playing and I'll be here to set the bones." We can choose not to risk the broken bones—or the failures, or the set-backs—but then we never get the joy of playing football, or breaking through in new areas in our life.

It's inevitable: we will fail at our efforts sometimes—maybe even many times. Remember Thomas Edison? When asked how he felt about failing to invent the light bulb for so long he replied, "I have not failed. I've just found 10,000 ways that do not work." Failure is inevitable when we're taking risks. What matters is our response to those failures. We need to recognize that the process of growth and achievement often involves failed attempts, requiring we get back up, evaluate what we can try differently, and keep going.

Our calling is *not* guaranteed to be easy. Just because our calling may be in an area of natural gifts and abilities doesn't mean we won't have to work hard. Even if we are exactly where God wants us to be, we cannot expect it to be free from obstruction. We'll have mornings where we don't want to get out of bed, and face opposition when we're trying to do something right. Often, we will face rejection, but each obstacle then changes into an opportunity to become more like our Lord.

Your vocational calling is *not* your identity. My friend, Siri, explains it this way, "God's calling on our lives is perfect, but this is an imperfect world. So to think that an imperfect job or place is our identity is wrong."

The reality is that our identity is in Christ, an identity not based on what we do, but who we are as children of God. We are called to Him daily, regardless of where we spend our working lives. And that calling is one that is only possible because of the price He paid on the cross, one that gives us the deepest gladness we will ever know.

PERSONAL REFLECTION: Your holistic calling does not change nor does your identity in Christ, even if your job does. Let that truth be the "one thing" that drives your passion.

Do you tie your identity too closely to a vocational calling? How would you feel if your job changed? How can you live out the reality of Christ's hope in you, knowing your vocation may change over time? If you haven't ever written your life mission statement, consider writing one now. As you do, ask God to help you see your present career as an opportunity to worship Him with the skills He's given you so that you can participate with Him to create meaningful change in the world.

PART II: GETTING REAL

conversations about the
challenges we face at work

CHAPTER 5

The Only One in the Room

I was in a "senior manager" meeting at work. The meeting consisted of our director, the eight or so leaders in our division, and the director's executive assistant. Besides me, the executive assistant was the only other woman in the room. Like many women I know, at the majority of the meetings I've attended since I started my career over a decade ago, most of my bosses, colleagues and clients have been men.

In my career I've worked mainly in the defense sector, which is known for being predominantly male. But even in sectors like education, health care, and non-profit organizations, the leadership tends to be male. Subsequently, in a lot of professional settings we may find ourselves as the only woman (or one of the few women) in the room.

Like many things in life, being the only woman in the room has both advantages and disadvantages. In my experience, sometimes being a woman has not been a big deal; other times I've received favoritism, and sometimes, although rarely, I've been subjected to sexual harassment. For many women, the fear of being (or appearing) too sensitive or emotional can be great.

But ironically, in some cases, the gift of sensitivity, which—let's face it—not everyone possesses, can be a strategic advantage.

Exploring the Christian Perspective

As I began research for this book, I found a lot of good advice in the various articles and books available for "surviving in a man's world" (because business has historically been perceived to be a man's domain). As I began writing this chapter, I wasn't sure how to differentiate my views from that of any other woman who writes about how to assert herself in meetings, or how to handle inappropriate colleagues. What then, I began to wonder, is unique about the perspective of a Christian woman? As we continue to wrestle with this idea of work and/or calling, what is a *Christian* woman to do when she's the only one in the room?

Thankfully, Scripture offers some guidance. In fact, Paul outlined some radical ideas about gender in Galatians 3. In writing to the Galatians about the difference between living under the Old Testament law and the New Testament Promise, Paul said, *So in Christ Jesus you are all children of God through faith, for all of you who were baptized into Christ have clothed yourselves with Christ. There is neither Jew nor Gentile, neither slave nor free, nor is there male and female, for you are all one in Christ Jesus. If you belong to Christ, then you are Abraham's seed, and heirs according to the promise,* (Galatians 3:26-29 NIV).

In Paul's day Jews were thought to be better than Greeks, free people were perceived as being superior to slaves, and men were valued far above women. In Galatians 3, Paul is saying that in God's ultimate plan, we will not rank ourselves according to those lines; we will instead understand that in God's eyes we are not loved any more or less because of our gender or ethnicity or socio-economic status. And in eternity, that will be true. But one of our jobs as believers is to bring God's kingdom of justice and mercy here to earth.

That doesn't mean we should overlook the unique characteristics of each person, or how their personalities have been shaped by their gender, race or the experience of their socioeconomic status. It does mean that we as Christians can view ourselves and others as equally valuable. If we approach our work environment perceiving ourselves as a peer to all colleagues, we create opportunities for meaningful dialogue. And whether male or female, if we act respectfully toward our employees or our bosses, we convey a portion of God's kindness toward His people.

But this type of Kingdom approach in the workplace requires humility. The word 'humble' is often misinterpreted. People tend to think of humble people as timid, lowly or docile. In actuality, humble means having a right understanding of oneself: an accurate consciousness of our gifts and abilities. Put differently: modesty. Humility includes our gifts as well as our weaknesses.

Jesus was humble and He certainly wasn't lowly or untalented or overly apprehensive. He knew He was the Son of God, but did not presume to make Himself better than others. He recognized and used His talents, not to diminish the humanity of others, but to encourage it. Jesus did not consider His equality with God something to be used or taken advantage of (Philippians 2:5-8); rather He made Himself nothing by taking the form of a servant, and became obedient to the cross.

In other words, being humble does not mean servile or out of touch; rather it reflects an understanding that our gifts came from a generous God, and were developed through His gift of the Holy Spirit shaping our work ethic. Humility—or an accurate perception of who we are and who we aren't in God's sight—actually makes us more secure because we no longer look to others for affirmation. We find our acceptance through Christ's work on the cross.

What happens when we bring into the workplace perspectives that include a right understanding of our strengths—and weaknesses—combined with the humility of a redeemed child of God? Those insights allow us to approach our work environment with confidence, respect, and integrity. It doesn't matter if we're a man or a woman. If we rightly understand the gifts and talents God gave us, and view ourselves and others through the promise of Galatians 3, we can enter our workplace as a peer to all, and humbly offer the skills God has given us for His service.

Nonetheless, while having this right understanding of ourselves is important for all Christians, it seems women are often more unsure of our role when "navigating a man's world." We struggle with church, marital and cultural norms of male leadership and don't know how to "assert ourselves" in the workplace without appearing disrespectful. Subsequently, it's a challenge to know if we stand up for ourselves enough, or too much; if we're being discriminated against because we're women, or because we just don't have the skills necessary to perform the job.

Navigating the Work Place

Even if we agree with the biblical message of humility and calling, we may not be sure how to put it into practice. Let's face it: being a woman in a male-dominated environment is an up and down struggle. Cultural influences gnaw at us, sometimes tempting us to ignore or question scriptural truth or to react to people and situations in ways that do not glorify God.

I've personally found it helpful to determine specific and practical steps to take that will enable me to respond appropriately when faced with unique challenges at work. And I believe that if we each think about the following areas in advance, we can be better prepared during those times we encounter similar situations:

Asserting Yourself. Let's revisit the senior managers meeting I talked about at the beginning of the chapter. I wasn't invited to the meeting when I first joined this company. About two months into the job I was asked to cover the meeting in the absence of a colleague who had the same responsibilities as I did, just for the week he was out of the office. Once invited, I suddenly realized that he's at the same position level that I am, and he's here. Shouldn't I be as well?

Paranoia moved through my head: why hadn't they asked me in the first place? Would I be perceived as pushy if I went? Would others consider me insecure if I asked if I could go? Or maybe I was not talented enough. I carried on an internal debate, second-guessing my abilities, and re-assessing my own strengths along with what I had to offer to the meeting. Then I considered the personalities of the men in the room and reminded myself of my worth as one for whom Jesus died. I decided to take a proactive and gentle step toward inclusion.

The next week I stood up straight and started attending the weekly meetings. Soon, my presence became accepted as the norm; in fact, I became more knowledgeable about the office, which has allowed me to contribute even more. Had I not asserted myself, I would have fallen "behind" my male colleagues who were at the meetings, learning about our strategic direction and responding to opportunities. And my colleagues would have missed out on the contributions I brought to the table.

Sheryl Sandberg, the Chief Operating Officer of Facebook, often encourages women to "sit at the table." In a TED— Thoughts, Entertainment and Design—talk in December 2010, she said that one of the most important things women can do to progress their professional development is to physically sit at the table. Too many times in meetings she's seen—and I have too—women take one of the chairs at the side of the room, which literally takes them out of the conversation. I'm sure a combination of factors has created this subservient view of ourselves; even so, I believe we must stop being so insecure about our role as a contributor to our businesses. Imagine what could happen if we began to speak up, rather than yielding to fear?!

Acting as Administrative Assistant: Another struggle many women have is how to strike a balance between serving others and being a doormat. While all Christians should look for ways to follow the example of servant leadership modeled by Jesus, I do notice a lot more women than men "volunteering for administrative functions"—i.e., caring for guests, taking notes during a meeting, etc. Yes, we are trying to be helpful, trying not to get caught up in the "whose turn is it?" or "not my job" games, and wanting to be a team player. But unless we were hired to be an administrative assistant, spending the majority of our time doing administrative functions is actually not being a servant leader because it likely means we are neglecting the job we were hired to do.

Conquering the Daughter Syndrome. Often, at the early stages of our careers, the men we work with are older than we are, and so it is not uncommon for a colleague to have a daughter our age. One of my friends, for instance, had a boss who mentioned her similarity to his daughters more than once—occasionally patting her on the head when he visited her desk and squeezing her knee when he sat down by her in a meeting. She honestly did not think he was being sexually inappropriate, but it still made her feel awkward, especially since she'd never seen him give a fatherly pat to any of the young men in their office. She wondered what the other men in her office thought when he squeezed her knee—did they think she was less professional? Or did they think she was taking advantage of the fact that she reminded him of his daughters?

Sure, sometimes it's nice when we have a special relationship with our colleagues or superiors. After all, relationships make the world go 'round, maybe even more than money! Professional relationships with mentors and sponsors are invaluable to our growth, but favoritism that is primarily attributed to gender— rather than ability—is confusing for everyone. When the tone of the relationship is more personal than professional, we are left to wonder if the other person recognizes our abilities, or just thinks we're a nice person. More significantly, we may struggle to get them to take our recommendations seriously.

I think men don't always intend to minimize our professional roles, but they do. My friend took an indirect approach to her situation; she sat in a chair across the room from the man so he couldn't pat her leg. It worked for her in that situation but if changing seats hadn't worked, a private, sincere discussion with this fatherly type co-worker would have been in order.

Recognizing Sexual Harassment. There's misguided fatherly affection from a kind, older colleague, and then there's flat out sexual harassment. I had heard about "hostile workplaces" but couldn't believe they actually existed until I faced it myself. How naïve I was.

When I first arrived at a six-month overseas assignment, I was warned by the male colleague from D.C. who I was replacing that there were a lot of things that went on in this department that I probably won't like. He also warned that if I were overly sensitive I'd "ruin" the relationship between our office and this one. I don't remember exactly how I responded, but it was along the lines of, "Whatever. I'm not that sensitive." I prided myself on not being easily offended and was confident I could handle the situation.

And then I had my first few days on the job. Except for the executive assistant, the entire staff was male. Many were there as bachelors, either "actual" bachelors or "geographical bachelors," a term used to describe men who were married but were on assignment without their spouse. These men often used their overseas opportunities for recreation, and using the city as their playground, regularly visiting strip clubs and prostitutes. While I found that behavior offensive, I didn't feel it was my role to criticize what they did in their personal time.

But their activities didn't stay in their personal time; they were all over the office. Too many times during "storytelling hour" they talked about their visits to strip clubs, or told crude jokes and sent inappropriate email forwards to me, so that eventually the entire office would see the pornography they looked at on company computers.

Then it got worse. Not long after I arrived, I became a subject of their attention. One superior used inappropriate text messages to express his interest in me, and I received regular advances from other men around the facility.

My first approach was light-hearted dismissal, implying that I didn't like their behavior. That didn't work. Then I expressed my concerns to another supervisor who was unwilling or unable to stop the behavior. I approached the security unit, and they sent me to the Equal Employment Opportunity Officer, who was the text sender's girlfriend. It was not exactly a well-received conversation.

I endured the length of my assignment and when I returned home I attempted to bring resolution. However, when I submitted formal complaints to my organization, I was transferred from one office to the next, each one telling me they were sorry, but it was not their responsibility. My boss' solution? To transfer me to another team and to no longer send women on that particular short-term assignment.

Ultimately, I decided the best thing for me to do was to change jobs completely. Some may criticize me for giving up too easily, but I could no longer accept the personal toll it was taking on my life. I lost sleep, lost weight, and suffered constant anxiety, all of which contributed to decreased productivity in my work (and life!).

Experiences and decisions like these can be very personal. If I were in that situation today, I don't know that I would have "gutted through" my assignment. I was afraid to say, "Yes, it *is* that bad" and didn't have the courage to leave. But I also don't think I would have given up so quickly on my attempts to lodge formal complaints and ensure they were resolved. If this field had been my ultimate passion, I would have just been shut out of it, especially because my office decided not to send any more women on this assignment. A mentor at the time encouraged me "not to meet trouble half way" and to stick with my convictions, but it was too late by then. I was exhausted.

If we decide to confront harassment like this, we should be prepared for a grueling emotional and physical toll. Two things helped me cope: a woman on the compound overseas who had experienced similar environments gave me the invaluable practical advice to, "document, document, document." Whenever something inappropriate happened I would write down what was going on around me—jokes told, activities referenced, advances by colleagues. This allowed me to remove myself from the situation and look at their behavior objectively. Writing everything down also gave me the "evidence" I needed when I lodged a formal complaint.

What was most valuable for me in that experience, though, was God's grace—shown to me through my dear friend Gayle. Never once did she doubt what I was going through; in fact, she made my mental health a priority in the midst of a busy time in her life. She offered to pray for me, and then she prayed, prayed, and prayed some more, with me and for me, throughout my assignment and after I returned home.

Working as women in male-dominated cultures inevitably means we will encounter unfortunate and sometimes damaging situations. When they happen, we do have options for fighting back. We must first learn to live in the tension of serving God's kingdom and asserting ourselves for His purposes. We must also learn to document, document, document, and to pray, pray, pray just as much, if not more. If push comes to shove, we can and must file a formal complaint for the sake of equity and justice for other women who might come after us, following it as far as our endurance allows us. Of course, in a situation of sexual harassment, it's crucial to get help and develop a support system to sustain us.

We know it is not easy navigating corporate settings that have been historically governed by men. But as we respond to God's call for our professional lives, we can be confident of this: we will never be alone in the room. The Lord Almighty is with us.

PERSONAL REFLECTION: All of these situations stress the importance of having a *right understanding of who you are*. What talents has God created in you that are useful in the workplace? How can you navigate your role with grace and strength, while exhibiting and earning respect? Ask God to guide you into nurturing support systems where you commit to praying for each other.

CHAPTER 6

The Men We Work With

Not long ago, three dear girlfriends of mine, all committed Christians, found themselves in inappropriate relationships with male colleagues. One friend, a married woman, had a relationship with a co-worker that turned into an emotional affair. Another friend, also married, had a brief physical encounter with a co-worker while on travel and had to face the aftermath of her actions. The last, an unmarried woman, was challenged by a relationship with her superior. It wasn't really "wrong," but she knew it wasn't right either.

As I learned of each of their dilemmas, my initial reaction was: *What?! How did three Christian women all get themselves into these situations? Did they* really *know and love God? How could this have happened?*

But these thoughts were short-lived. I quickly remembered my own sinful nature: yes, godly women do fall. When we're "in the world" we can expect temptations. But was it just my friends and me who encountered these situations? Why hadn't anyone told us of the temptations that might come as a result of working alongside men? I am certain other Christian women are not immune to these struggles, but it can be difficult to talk about the experience.

But we must. Why? Because navigating relationships with colleagues of the opposite sex is another area that can present a challenge for Christian professionals. We can't just strategize about how to assert ourselves in our working environment, like we discussed in the last chapter, but we also must examine the sometimes romantic tensions of male/female relationships.

No matter what we might think, these things happen. In the world, we *will* struggle with how to interact appropriately with our male colleagues, and we *will* face temptation. No matter where we work, we need to be prepared for what we might face and how to stand strong, if we are going to establish mature and appropriate relationships with our male colleagues. If we haven't considered what boundaries to put in place, it's important to consider them now.

Define *Appropriate and Inappropriate* for Me, Please

Some of us might be unsure about what it means to be *appropriate*, so here's my own definition: to enjoy an *appropriate* relationship with someone of the opposite sex is to honor God, our spouse and the other person's spouse, and to exhibit behavior that reflects a Christ-like character. As Paul writes in 1 Peter, *"As He who called you is holy, you also be holy in all your conduct,"* (1:15 NKJV).

When men and women—who are both made in God's image and yet sinful—come together in the same environment, their interactions with one another can span the gamut. There can be creative and professional chemistry that is highly positive and productive, or there can be power struggles that are highly negative and ineffective. But what happens when the interactions blur the line from *professional* to *personal*? Or when things get too friendly, which can also lead to ineffectiveness in our work?

Let's start with a short quiz. I've spoken to a number of friends about what they consider to be "borderline" behavior, or situations that have led to temptation. They responded with the items on the list below. Let's consider honestly whether we have engaged in the following with a male co-worker:

- Shared personal information to the point of creating intimate friendships with male co-workers;
- Sent suggestive non-verbal messages, however subtle or overt, through interpersonal communication, (i.e. looks, expressions, physical touch, even clothing choices);
- Thought of a male colleague's reaction when making wardrobe selections;
- Communicated about subjects beyond work after business hours;
- Emailed or instant messaged a colleague about specific personal matters;
- Looked too long (stared) at a colleague who we found attractive;
- If married, complained about or demeaned your spouse to a colleague;
- Participated in a long conversation about a male colleague's wife or personal life;
- Traveled for work with just another male colleague, especially late-night working dinners;

- Outright flirted, expressed suggestive comments, or said anything we wouldn't say or write in front of fellow church members or spouse.

I'll admit, I had a negative reaction to a number of things on this list. I felt like their points were a bit legalistic. I argued that I wasn't sure what was wrong with sharing personal information with a male colleague, especially if I'm around that person *all day*—longer than I am around anyone else (including my spouse): was I supposed to be a robot? Just talk about the weather? I also wondered how I could avoid working one-on-one with male colleagues if it's part of my *job*. Was I supposed to bring a third person on travel, when the project budget would not realistically allow it?

My friends were quick to point out that these things are not inherently wrong, but too often, they were the open door that led to a relationship they later realized wasn't healthy.

As with many temptations, there is sometimes a rush of excitement that accompanies seemingly harmless behavior. Interaction and attention are flattering, but they also can entice bad decisions. So how do we stop our own questionable behavior? Or how do we stop it when we're on the receiving end of this type of unwanted behavior? The key is to decide in advance what constitutes appropriate and inappropriate behavior, so we can recognize when we *first* begin to slip and get accountability from a trusted friend. (As an aside, for those of us who are married, our spouse may not be the best accountability partner in this situation, but we should be transparent about what is happening.)

It may seem easier to ignore temptation when it first seems small or even "manageable"—particularly in the workplace where there is an expectation of professionalism. We don't want to "make a big deal" out of "nothing." But in the Song of Solomon, these types of small problems within a romantic relationship are referred to as little foxes (v. 2:15). Whether we are married or single, the imagery is appropriate: the foxes crept into vineyards and destroyed the vines by gnawing on the root. These little foxes of inappropriate relationships will dig away at the root structures: the root structure of our relationship with God, our relationships with others, and potentially with our spouse or future spouse.

"But It's Not a Sin for Me!"

The point of examining these potential dangers in gender relations at work is to be alert to the possibilities, even if we think, "that would never happen to me." What seem to be small issues can often grow into big ones. And one of the "bigger" areas of concern in the Bible is adultery. It's one of the original 10 commandments or "rules" God gave us, the seventh in a set of crucial mandates Moses receives from God in Exodus 20:14. It might seem ironic, but those commandments actually show us God's design for a life of freedom, that is, a life free from harming ourselves and our loved ones.

Here's what I mean: We are not called to be robots who blindly do whatever we're told, but neither should we seek intimacy from inappropriate places. And it's important to ask ourselves how many men we want to have emotional intimacy with. The answer to that question for me is "as few as possible."

But I also know that spending a lot of time with a person can create the appearance (in our eyes, or the eyes of others) of a relationship that simply doesn't exist. For instance, do you know where the idea of mermaids came from? When sailors were spending all their time at sea, manatees started looking like beautiful women—hence, the illusion of mermaids. When we're sharing Chinese takeout with a colleague four nights of the week to meet a deadline, he can become the recipient of the after-work conversation we would otherwise share with our spouse or another good friend. And without even expecting it, this guy can suddenly turn into a "merman." Although this individual is someone to whom we would not normally be attracted, we can be drawn to him because of the lack of attention we've given the intimacy in our other relationships. Long working hours, in other words, can take their toll in more ways than one.

And this is how scandal begins. A scandal isn't just a disgraceful event; it's the appearance and/or allegations of wrongdoing, whether true or false. If our behavior creates a scandal—even the *appearance* of wrongdoing—without actually engaging in any "wrong" behavior, then we are likely heading in the wrong direction.

Jesus gives us a clear warning in Matthew 5:27-28: "You have heard that it was said, 'You shall not commit adultery.' But I tell you that anyone who looks at a woman lustfully has already committed adultery with her in his heart," (NIV). If we are coveting our colleagues' attention, if we are building a deep personal relationship with them that does not belong in the work environment, we must ask ourselves if we are really reserving our heart for God? Or for our spouse? Or getting in the way of our colleague reserving his heart for his spouse?

Our Personality

Close proximity, project deadlines and other factors can certainly affect how we respond to the opposite sex while at work. But another question is important to ask: What kind of personality do we display at work? Though some of us might see ourselves as shy or modest in some environments, perhaps another personality manifests itself when we interact with our male colleagues. We might convey an altogether different persona at work, ranging from mature or motherly to flirty or friendly. Asking this question can help encourage sincere, objective self-examination.

If we're not sure what we're like at work, though, we should waste no time asking someone. It's important that each of us reach out to a mentor or another female colleague to give us feedback about a range of our behavior and abilities that we might not see ourselves. While a naturally expressive and outgoing woman can be excellent at creating rapport with clients and colleagues, she can also find herself misunderstood or, to put it more candidly, viewed as flirtatious. Knowing how our co-workers—both male and female—might interpret our behavior could be an eye-opening—and humbling—experience.

Regardless of whether we are outgoing or reserved, we are responsible for the signals we send. Now, I understand that this may seem a bit unfair. How can we *possibly* be responsible for the thoughts and reactions of men, particularly those who don't even aspire to godly standards? But that's not what I said; I said that we are responsible for our own *behavior*, which has a great deal to do with how men view us. In the Christian community we talk about not causing others to "stumble. "

And in Romans 14:13 Paul reminds us to be conscious of the consequences of our choices and behavior on those around us. If we want to be salt and light in the workplace, we need to be aware if others regularly perceive our behavior as a distraction.

Our Actions Have Consequences

A friend of mine—I'll call her Bethany—and her male colleague exchanged friendly emails at work. The emails got longer and more personal over the course of a few weeks. Bethany enjoyed the attention she was getting from her co-worker, especially because her husband was consumed with a graduate school program and had little free time to spend with her. Almost immediately Bethany felt like her colleague knew more about her than her husband did. Bethany even felt a little entitled to the attention, since she felt like her husband was neglecting her.

Then one day, her husband accidently came across one of the email exchanges between Bethany and her colleague. Bethany told me it was devastating. Her husband felt betrayed, and that he had failed her in ways he could have never imagined. While some people may view the exchange as minor—they were just emails, after all—Bethany saw the look on her husband's face and said there was nothing she regretted more. A few years later, Bethany and her husband are still rebuilding their trust.

Another friend—let's call her Katie—started working late with one of her colleagues who was married. Katie felt like she was learning a lot professionally and was hesitant to put up roadblocks even though the relationship felt, in her mind, "borderline inappropriate." Then the unthinkable happened, and when she least expected it; their relationship became physical. Katie knew what she was doing was wrong, but she admitted that she was flattered by his affection and didn't have anyone else in her life who was so attentive to her. As a result, Katie began to push away friends and stopped attending Bible study because she didn't want to let people know what was really going on in her life. Sadly, she said she also withdrew from God because she knew she was sinning but at the same time, she didn't want to stop. Consequently, Katie felt like she couldn't legitimately approach God.

"Amy"—another friend about my age—also became physically involved with a man at her work—only in Amy's situation, it was with her boss. She didn't feel it was wrong—they were both single adults who had a lot in common. And to avoid any appearance of impropriety, they kept their relationship a secret. But when one of her boss's superiors found out, he reported them for violating the organization's policy on relationships between supervisors and employees. Both Amy and her boss were reprimanded and had notes put in their personnel files.

When we engage in these kinds of relationships—as Bethany, Katie and Amy all found out—we put not just our character on the line, but our jobs. Our professionalism is compromised as well as our relationships with our friends, our spouse, and ultimately, our God. The stakes are simply too high to allow even a tiny door to open toward improper situations.

Drastic Measures

If we do find ourselves in an inappropriate relationship and we are in over our head because of either the emotional or physical component, there's no simple solution: *drastic action is required!* Anyone who has spent time in Scripture knows that when God wants to emphasize a critical point, He repeats it several times, and often with great emphasis. Consider, for instance, Christ's sobering words in Matthew 5:29 and 18:9 (NKJV) when he teaches on adultery: " . . . If your eye causes you to stumble, gouge it out and throw it away. It is better for you to enter life with one eye than to have two eyes and be thrown into the fire of hell."

Sinning with lust through the eyes is indistinguishable from actual adultery; to God they are the *same* offense. The dramatic image of cutting out one's eye is intended to provoke a dramatic response and a turning away from such sin. Some of us—like "Amy"— may not *want* to make drastic changes to such a relationship because it is gratifying to us, or because it would be awkward professionally. We may even try to justify such an affair, regardless of whether it's emotional or physical. But the painful reality—and it *is* ultimately painful—confirms that sin *always* has negative consequences. Period. If we are struggling in any way with an improper relationship, we must run—fast and far—like Joseph did from Potiphar's wife (Genesis 39)!

Good News: There *Are* Constructive Professional Male/Female Relationships!

What if we're *not* in a situation where we know we're in over our head? What if we haven't encountered flirty colleagues or fallen into the temptations like I described above?

First, I'll say, "Well done!" It's probably no accident when any of us don't find ourselves in these situations. That might be in part because we don't *need* to "run" from healthy relationships with colleagues or look at every man with fear of the relationship turning unhealthy.

So if we have already established boundaries around our behavior and relationships at work, we can appreciate the varied contributions our male co-workers make without feeling compromised. The important thing is to establish those limits long *before* we need them. Then we can share them with someone who can keep us accountable to honoring the commitments we've made to God, our spouse, and ourselves.

The good news is that men and women really can be effective co-workers, and when they are, the workplace is all the more interesting, productive and valuable. Instead of removing themselves from the office or refusing to work with men, women can take heart, trust God and find common ground. Besides, when either women or men refuse to work with the opposite sex—and both scenarios make my blood boil!—it's nothing short of discriminatory, advancing neither their company's goals nor their own personal ones.

Obviously, we will have things in common with the people we work with, and getting to know them, building friendships as well as professional relationships, can be a good thing. There really are plenty of healthy male/female relationships out there, fulfilling strategic goals, honoring the unique giftedness of the other and maintaining integrity in the process. We just need to be on guard against the unhealthy and unproductive ones.

PERSONAL REFLECTION: Appropriate relationships with the men in our offices requires prayer, wisdom and commitment to doing the right thing—long before the wrong thing might sneak up on us. Revisit the quiz mentioned early in this chapter. In what ways might you need to work on more appropriate interactions? How can you deliberately honor your colleagues while not compromising professionalism? Ask God to help you set boundaries and to provide a friend or mentor to hold you accountable to those. And celebrate the healthy relationships you do have!

CHAPTER 7

Why Morals Matter

Choosing Integrity and Living Above Reproach

Above all else, guard your heart, for everything you do flows from it (Prov. 4:23, NIV)

The West Point Code of Honor includes the statement: "Do not lie, cheat or steal, nor tolerate those who do." After I heard that, I thought I'd consider what that looked like in my own life. I'm not sure why the exercise intrigued me, I didn't really consider myself a liar, a cheater or a thief, but I asked God to reveal to me areas where I might be unaware. I wanted Him to check my conscience.

Was I in for a surprise! "Sorry, I am late, traffic was horrible." (Well, actually I didn't want to get out of bed and I just lied to you.) "I spent about 16 hours on that project." (I spent about 11 hours working on it, and about two hours on the Internet and three hours doing who knows what—I'm stealing from you.) "Wow, I sure am glad the cop caught the car in front of me." (I was going 20 miles over the speed limit—I was cheating.)

It's the Little Things

We may think the examples above are "minor infractions." Or because "everybody else is doing it," we can as well. After all, I don't lie on my taxes and I don't rob banks. On *my* scale from zero to murder, the things I listed above are about a .025.

But does God measure our sin on a scale like that? There are certainly different consequences depending on the severity of the sin, but is any sin "minor" when it is committed against a loving and holy God?

Besides, the Bible doesn't say, "It's okay, as long as you can be trusted with the big things." In fact, it says the exact opposite. In Luke 16:10-12 (NIV), Jesus is speaking to His disciples about stewardship and tells the story of a debt collector who worked for a rich man. The debt collector gets "creative" in collecting his master's debts and Jesus says, "Whoever can be trusted with very little can also be trusted with much, and whoever is dishonest with very little will also be dishonest with much."

His point? If we can't be trustworthy in handling worldly wealth, how can we be trusted with true riches? And if we have not been trustworthy with someone else's property, how can we be trusted with property of our own?

The way we handle even seemingly insignificant matters defines both our integrity and our professionalism. When I demonstrate that I can be trusted with the "little" things, like being honest with my co-workers about why I'm late or telling the truth on my timesheet, I feel like I'm in a better position to try to tackle the "big" things I want to be able to do.

How the Mighty Fall

As I write this, a popular politician has been blasted in the news for an extra-marital affair. Another is facing heat for inappropriate pictures of himself that are circulating. Well-known and trusted bankers are caught feeding their clients deals that all-but-guarantee they'll lose money.

Sadly, there is no shortage of examples these days of "how the mighty have fallen." Plenty of people serve an important function in our country as role models because of their athletic or leadership abilities or show business success, yet have made some serious—and very public—moral missteps.

We look at these people and wonder how they could do these things. We also get a little self-righteous that at least we weren't that dumb (or at least haven't been caught being that dumb). We often wonder if they can be trusted to do their jobs. Other times we're more compassionate, knowing they're just regular people and shouldn't be put on a pedestal.

But is it only the mighty who have fallen? Is it only the famous or non-Christians who cheat on their spouses or lie on their taxes? Of course not. A woman I know through church had an extra-marital affair with a man from her gym. It wasn't all over the news, but it happened. Several years ago another woman, who had attended our neighborhood church for years and served in many ministry roles, was convicted of embezzling from the church when she served as the treasurer.

Obviously, we are human, which also means we are sinners. That's why committing ourselves to principles of integrity is important in our work as well as our witness as Christians. How, though, do we deal with our own sinfulness in the office?

Morality on the Job

It used to be that the requirement for a job was intelligence or plain old book smarts. Then people started talking about emotional intelligence, that to succeed we had to know how to build relationships and communicate well. Lately, I've seen a new term crop up in career resources: moral intelligence. Now employers must spell out their expectation for what was once considered a standard part of any job: character. Today's professional must know how to live and work by some generally accepted ethical boundaries, such as integrity, responsibility, forgiveness, and compassion.

Business leaders are wondering about this when they are hiring. And with good reason: a company's entire accounting practices, for instance, are called into question after one senior vice president is convicted of embezzlement. When members of a government agency are found to be hiring escorts and throwing wild parties, it usually leads to a large-scale investigation into whether these problems are endemic, or just isolated incidents. So employers understandably have to question if they can trust their employees because the organization's reputations are on the line.

But let's not forget that our own reputation is on the line, too. Do I want to be known as the woman who will do *anything* necessary to get a promotion? Do I want others to remember me for my "creative accounting skills" that somehow always balanced the books? Am I that woman who is too busy checking Facebook to get her job done?

Even more important than that, as Christians in the workplace, God's reputation is on the line. How we behave reflects on Him. And I admit that sometimes it seems unfair—we are ridiculous representations of Him at times. But Paul writes in 2 Corinthians 3:2-3 that we are sent from Christ: *You yourselves are our letter, written on our hearts, known and read by everyone. You show that you are a letter from Christ, the result of our ministry, written not with ink but with the Spirit of the living God, not on tablets of stone but on tablets of human hearts* (NIV).

We are what people read and learn about God, so our behavior at work, and in life, is important. Our behavior is the most obvious part of that letter written with the Spirit of the living God.

How Should We Behave?

As Christians, our moral guidelines are found in the Bible. In the first book of Timothy, Paul describes the qualities the Church should look for in leaders. He writes of the concept of *living above reproach* (1 Tim 3:2) and uses words like "self-controlled, honest, hospitable, able to teach, not given to drunkenness." He goes on to say they "must also have a good reputation with outsiders so that he will not fall into disgrace and into the devil's trap."

It's not unreasonable to think those guidelines are good for all Christians and for leaders outside the Church. But that list, and other words found in the Bible, like "blameless" or "pure in heart" can feel a bit intimidating if we try to create our own "righteousness."

That's why we need a Savior! Living a "blameless" life is about letting Christ's life spill out of us as an example for others. As we do, we become the type of person who can be counted on to advocate for what is right and to oppose what is wrong. It's about establishing trust so that people know they can count on us. Most people would say they want this of their colleagues, but as Christians, it can feel like an even weightier responsibility.

Maybe it feels weightier because we hear a lot of Christian leaders speak from the pulpit, stage or page and say, "No excuses, you should never compromise your moral values for a job." In theory, I agree. In practice, it's not always that simple, and few publically acknowledge that.

But I confess I have lied at my job. I've gossiped, I've been unkind, I have had too much to drink at the work holiday party, resulting in poor decision-making, and I've thought I was "above the rules." And I'm guessing I'm not alone.

More than once after I've behaved like an arrogant jerk, a selfish brat or a cutthroat at work, I've worried about what my colleagues will think of Christians. At other times I've been glad no one *really* knew I was a Christian. In other words, I know my behavior—from the small things to the big—reflects on God, and I'm not always proud of what I've done.

Even so, this is not a discussion about the "Christian to-do list"— or rather, the "Christian to-don't list." Instead, I believe the focus for believers is not on a keeping a bunch of rules, but on our heart. If our hearts are centered on Christ, our behavior will follow, starting with the smallest issue that might just affect us (i.e., why I was really late to work) to the areas that have far bigger consequences on those around us (i.e., stealing from corporate accounts).

I think the Amplified version of Luke 6:45 describes this heart/behavior connection well: "*The upright (honorable, intrinsically good) man out of the good treasure [stored] in his heart produces what is upright (honorable and intrinsically good), and the evil man out of the evil storehouse brings forth that which is depraved (wicked and intrinsically evil); for out of the abundance (overflow) of the heart his mouth speaks."* And since all of our behaviors reflect our hearts, it's essential to understand what is really going on, that is, to take an honest account of what our behavior looks like so we'll get a clearer picture of what's inside us.

Not Sinning in the First Place

The easiest way to get out of any sin predicament—"major" or "minor"—is to not get into it in the first place. Think about David – he was the young man who defeated the towering Philistine Goliath, he became King of Jerusalem, and he had the privilege of being an ancestor to Jesus Christ.

But he was also known for his murderous affair with Bathsheba. David could have looked away from Bathsheba's rooftop. Instead he chose to pursue his curiosity, ultimately killing Bathsheba's husband Uriah so that he could take her for himself.

"But David did so much good, too," you might rightfully point out. I completely agree. The point is, not only do the little sins fundamentally weaken your witness to those that know about them, but they can also lead to far greater personal failures. Nothing is outside the ability of God. He *can* redeem a broken life, failed marriage or ruined reputation. But doesn't it make a lot more sense (and save a lot more heartache) to CLING to the admonishments in Scripture that illustrate how to live above reproach?

When we are tempted to lie, cheat or steal, we need to ask ourselves what is controlling us. What makes us act a certain way? Competitiveness? Fear? Arrogance? Laziness? Is that what we want to control us? Or do we want to be controlled by the love of Christ?

Getting Away with it or Getting Caught

Prevention is great, but I'm not always successful at setting up boundaries to keep myself from sinning. (Sometimes I intentionally jump right over the boundaries!) And then, if no one "catches me," I think I've gotten away with it. But God still sees it.

We may think we get away with our sin at work because no one catches us lying on our timesheet, or in an affair with a colleague. But God knows. In Mark 3:5 we see Jesus distressed by our stubborn hearts. He sees it in our actions, and in our thoughts, and it grieves Him. The point? We don't ever "get away" with our sins where God is concerned. And, sometimes, we don't "get away with it" professionally either. So what happens when we "get caught?"

As an independent consultant, a friend was bidding on a new project and needed a current client to verify work she had completed. She wrote up an evaluation of her work and sent it off to her client for a signature. She knew that she had been a little generous as she recounted her work, but it was all "within the norms" of how these evaluations were written in her industry.

Her client called her on it. Very politely, and leaving her dignity intact, her client said, "I think you're stretching it" and declined to sign the evaluation without a revision. My friend was furious, but after a lot of prayer, she re-wrote the evaluation and submitted it again to her client. Her client signed it and my friend ended up winning a very large project even with the toned-down evaluation.

I asked her if winning the contract was the redeeming part of the story. She said the redeeming part was hearing God's voice remind her that He had already written her story. Even if she thought it was not good enough, she knew He was telling her, "it is better than you could ever imagine. You will win business based on the story I have given you – not one you think you can create.'"

How Do We Move on?

Perhaps we've gotten "caught" doing something we regretted, or are aware of some wrong behavior no one else has yet discovered. But the truth is, we are all sinners, so sooner or later—or frankly, every single day—we're going to do something that distorts God's image. What do we do about it?

We take responsibility for our mistakes. We confess our mistakes to God—who is faithful and just to forgive us. And if our mistake has been perpetrated against other people, we seek to make it right either through an apology or corrective action, and often both. Our first priority is to ask God to change our hearts and then we proactively set up boundaries in our lives to avoid making the same mistakes again. It's not easy, but it's part of the journey God has called us to.

I would love to tell you that I return to God every time I find myself out of line or zinged with the conviction of the

Holy Spirit about a misstep. Admittedly, I do not, but I have found that the more I do, I feel it honors the Lord and respects the person I have wronged. And, to be honest, it helps me. I don't like lingering guilt any more than the next person.

It's like telling the truth, or keeping yourself from stealing, or looking away when we'd rather swoon over a handsome colleague. Making these right decisions is a muscle we need to keep in shape. Dietrich Bonhoeffer, a well-known German pastor and theologian, said as much in his book *Ethics*: "Telling the truth is something which must be learnt."[13] If we're continually being dishonest, stealing, or cheating, it's hard to flex the "right" muscles. They feel odd and they don't work very well. But if we keep telling the truth, protecting our and God's reputations, it becomes easier to make the right decisions. As author John Maxwell put it, "Integrity is not a given factor in everyone's life. It is a result of self-discipline, inner trust, and a decision to be relentlessly honest in all situations."

Should I Stay or Should I Go?

By now, it's probably become clear that I've wanted to address sin and misbehavior in this chapter. And very often how we respond to our failures has more of an impact on others than how we respond to our successes. Even so, it's important to note that sometimes the failings are not our own, that they might belong to others in the organization for which we work.

Certain industries might have a reputation for being less-than-ethical. We should know that when we're considering our professional options or engaging in these businesses, that we're

---

[13] Dietrich Bonhoeffer, *Ethics*, page 360

going to encounter the darker sides of these occupations. And even the best organizations can slip under the influence of less-than-honorable leaders.

By now, it's safe to conclude that I believe Christians belong in practically any type of job. Too many times, though, we sit on the sidelines and fail to engage, but then lob all sorts of criticism at the "ridiculous politics" or the "garbage on television" or the "corrupt banking industry."

I've heard Christian leaders say things like, "If your job asks you to do something morally questionable, then leave. No job is worth your integrity." When I hear that I think to myself, "How morally questionable? Kill someone? Got it— no job is worth that." But how about those times we take off on a Thursday afternoon to go to a baseball game with our colleagues for office bonding and our boss tells us just to charge it as regular hours? Uhh . . .

The question came up for me when I was reading a profile in *Christianity Today* about Jeff Van Duzer, author of the book, *Why Business Matters to God: (And What Still Needs to be Fixed)*. Van Duzer wrote about the moral conundrums people sometimes face in the business world. I get it that he's not talking about baseball games and whether or not that is "stealing leave" from our company, because if I'm honest, I know that's a bad choice. But he clarified the tension we face really well:

> Christians can't accept a position of compromise until it is the very last option. They have to strain for that creative solution that allows them to do it all. Then, when they are absolutely

forced to choose the lesser of two evils, they have to acknowledge that nonetheless, they are choosing evil. That should call them to confession, repentance, and a deep longing for the day when we won't be living in this kind of world anymore.[14]

Van Duzer had the courage to acknowledge the tension we are operating in because we live in a fallen world. I'm not implying we should give up on living above reproach because it's just too hard. I am saying that, at times, we are going to have to make a decision where any of the options will have negative consequences. We need to make those decisions with God's guidance, through His word, prayer and wise counsel from friends we respect.

One Last Time: It's About Our Heart

Just like we're tempted to think that "balance" is (a) achievable and (b) will lead to unending bliss and sunshine, "living above reproach" by trying to keep all these rules, and enforce them on others, is not the secret to a perfect life. Thank goodness!

We can't dress up our sin and pretend it doesn't happen. Acting holy while hiding our sin is painful for us and for the people around us, especially when we lord our piety over them. Instead, we need to *let your adorning be the hidden person of the heart with the imperishable beauty of a gentle and quiet spirit, which in God's sight is very precious* (1 Peter 3:4 EVS).

---

[14] http://www.christianitytoday.com/ct/article_print.html?id=90655

The more we spend time in God's presence, the more His character and the values of His Kingdom shine through us to a world in need of both. We don't have to dress ourselves up or pretend we are any more or less than He has made us.

PERSONAL REFLECTION: Living above reproach is not about being sinless. It's not about walking around in a perpetual state of guilt for all the infractions we do everyday. It's about turning our hearts in toward Christ—acknowledging the sin that He points out to us, and correcting those errors, with His help. Let the Holy Spirit bring your killed off conscience back to life.

Ask God to point out where you're violating His code of conduct (not just West Point's) and then start behaving like a Christian: redeemed.

"Such confidence we have through Christ before God. Not that we are competent in ourselves to claim anything for ourselves, but our competence comes from God. He has made us competent as ministers of a new covenant—not of the letter but of the Spirit; for the letter kills, but the Spirit gives life." (2 Corinthians 3:4-6)

PART III: GETTING GOING
*ensuring our faith is present in every aspect
of our lives, including our jobs*

CHAPTER 8

A "For-Benefit" Life

*"You shall open wide your hand to your brother, to
the needy and the poor in your land"*
(Deuteronomy 15:11, ESV.)

It's one thing to confront the reality of interoffice dynamics,
as we did in the previous chapter. But it's an entirely different
challenge for us to think beyond our careers and into the world
around our office buildings.

If we live and work in urban settings, we probably see
economic disparities every day. We might pass homeless
women or housing projects and as we do, we remember that
not everyone has the same opportunities we've been given. That
fact is reinforced the minute we pick up a newspaper or go
online and see the challenges others face throughout the world.

So what does this have to do with our work? Much, if we
consider the more than 300 references on social justice and
treatment of the poor throughout the Old and New Testaments.
In fact, God's concern for the poor is obvious whenever we

open the Bible. He was concerned with the way His people were treated in Egypt in Deuteronomy 25:9. In Isaiah 41:17, he promised not to forsake those in need. In the Gospels, Jesus referred to how the poor (Luke 6:20-21), and the "poor in spirit" will be blessed (Matthew 5). But do we demonstrate the same attitude? Do we show concern for the poor? Are we indifferent to the poor, or concerned, but only from a distance?

If we take the Bible seriously, we know we're called to reflect God's compassion toward the poor. As Christians, we are called to *be* Christ to the poor. In Deuteronomy 15:7, Moses advised the Israelites not to harden their hearts or close their hands to the poor. And in Luke 3:11, John the Baptist told the crowds that if they have plenty, they are to share it with those who have nothing.

But who are "the poor" among us today? We are accustomed to thinking of the poor as those without money or options and that is a correct assessment. Neediness, though, encompasses a lack of all types of resources, not just financial. There are verses in the Bible in which God specifically refers to the poor as those without money. But the Bible also refers to people who are oppressed, who don't have freedom. The poor are those who are downtrodden. They have been hurt by life and need extra support. Whether we have financial, emotional, physical or spiritual resources, we are called to share them with those who do not.

So God's concern is clear and His instruction is clear, but how do we put it in action?

110

Serving in the Busyness

I'm busy. Personally, after working a long day, I feel like all I have time and energy to do is make dinner, eat dinner, and get ready for the next day. How on earth am I supposed to attend a Bible study, volunteer with my church's children's ministry, play on my alumni softball team, and do laundry? Oh, and take care of widows and orphans, the kind of religion that God says He accepts in James 1:27 (NIV)

Here is a bit of tough love: we're all busy, and we all make choices about how we spend our time. It can be hard to prioritize when everything we're doing is important. Bible studies, friends, and laundry are all important—but God gives us specific instructions in the Bible to make taking care of the poor one of our top priorities. So how can we make time in our lives to serve others? Many organizations, including churches, have occasional "service events" in which people gather together to volunteer at the neighborhood food pantry, or conduct a clothing drive for the local homeless families. So we add that event into our schedules and we're tempted to think that's "enough." The thought of adding more to our already-packed lives can be overwhelming. But if we look at our model for service—Jesus—we see a different perspective: Jesus didn't simply *participate* in service events; he demonstrated a *lifestyle* of serving.

"For-Benefit" Lifestyles

In our economy, we often divide organizations into three sectors: the "for-profit" sector which includes entities designed to provide goods or services, with the goal of making money;

the "non-profit" sector which is an entity that provides goods or services for the public and does not have the stated goal of producing a financial reward (or reinvests any financial reward to further their mission); and the "government" sector which furnishes goods and services to the community in return for taxes.

In recent years, a new sector has emerged. Some organizations have been doing this for a long time, but the idea is gaining traction as a way of doing business. Called the "for-benefit" sector, the guiding philosophy mixes business approaches with social interests. For-benefit organizations subscribe to a "triple bottom line"—not just focusing on the financial bottom line, but also the kind of impact the company is having on a social bottom line and an environmental bottom line. These are "blended value" organizations that don't tack a philanthropic effort onto their business model. They instead seek to make social change *through* their business model.

How could we apply that model to our lives so that we're not just operating in a "for-profit" mode when we're at work and a "non-profit" mode when we're at church? How can we better integrate the different parts of our lives and apply our professional skills to serve others, so we don't risk seeing our service get squeezed out when the allotted time runs slim?

Immediate thoughts go to "helping professions"—such as nursing or teaching—which seem more generous by their very nature. Nurses use their jobs to help those in need all the time, and they have a skill set that easily translates into volunteering; think of spending a few hours at a free clinic.

But stockbrokers can serve Christ just as effectively. How so? What if a broker convinced her bosses to donate three hours of her time every other week, so she could use her financial understanding to volunteer at an outreach center, teaching financial-literacy classes for high school students? What about an attorney? Instead of being an usher at church or volunteering with the children's ministry, a friend of mine volunteers with Christian Legal Aid, where she "defends the rights of the afflicted and the needy" (Jeremiah 22:16). Volunteering with our church's children's ministry is wonderful, but we can always use our professional skills to meet needs as well.

My church used to meet in Union Station in Washington, D.C., which is a gathering place for homeless people in the area. On Sundays a group of church members would hand out brown-bag lunches to people who congregated outside of Union Station—meeting a need while building deeper relationships. From that experience, my friend, John and I started "The Living Room," a weeknight gathering at which we studied the Bible and shared a meal with the homeless people we served on Sundays. I wanted to have a Bible study in my schedule, and this enabled me to use that time as an opportunity to also serve others.

John and I, along with the other "volunteers," became a part of an organic community of friends made up of people with and without homes; we all shared our concerns and our needs with one another. It wasn't just me serving someone—it was a "for-benefit" experience. I used my project management skills to organize our efforts, and I received fellowship and spiritual growth through these times. I also came to care deeply for these friends, and I felt their care for me.

Shouldn't Taking Care of the Poor be left to Professionals?

The needs of the poor can be overwhelming, and it's not uncommon for people to say they feel unequipped to deal with the range of problems—be it homelessness in our city or a family member's illness. I am grateful there are organizations with a mission to take care of the poor and help the sick.

While it is true that organizations dedicated to helping the poor are often more efficient and effective, the presence of formal programs—run by either non-profit organizations or the government—does not negate our personal responsibility and privilege, as Christians, to care for the poor. In Matthew 25, Jesus explains how when we give the hungry something to eat, the thirsty something to drink, when we visit the prisoner, we are giving to Him. We give to the hungry not to earn our salvation, but because we have been with our Savior and His kindness to us motivates our kindness to others.

How Do I Give and To Whom?

Our resources and capacity to serve are as unique as we are. We might have wonderful grandparents who are now gone, but we can still love the elderly. We can be intentional about connecting at a retirement home near work or home, stopping there for an hour every week for a game of cards. Or perhaps we have a brother who has struggled with a health issue; his children need rides to soccer practice or help with their homework on a school night. Our service to those around us in need doesn't have to be glamorous or grand. What is important is remembering the brokenhearted and making *their* care a part of our every day life.

My friend Lydia suggests that we ask the Lord to break our hearts for the unexpected. Our hearts can break for the missions videos we see at church, but, she says, if we keep our eyes open for the unexpected opportunities close to home, we will inevitably be led to be God's hands. And sometimes those things that look insignificant will mean the world to the person with the need. If you ask God to reveal needs to you, He will answer.

The Benefit's Reward

Our responsibility and privilege to share God's concern for the poor and serve them accordingly is clear. Figuring out how to do it, in the midst of the many demands on our time and energy, is complicated. But there's one more component in this outward-focused lifestyle: God's reward. While it shouldn't be our motivation, there are consequences for serving or not serving the poor.

God identifies penalties for oppressing or not serving the poor. In Ezekiel 22:31, He says He pours out His indignation on those who oppress the sojourner without justice, and in Matthew 25, He makes clear His judgment on those who neglect the hungry or homeless. In Luke 6:24, Jesus said those who don't take care of the poor are receiving their "comfort in full" now, implying this is all they'll get.

But the flip side of overlooking the marginalized is that in His Word, God associates spiritual and material reward with serving the poor. Consider the prophet Isaiah's words in chapter 58:10-11, some of my favorite verses addressing this issue:

If you spend yourselves in behalf of the hungry and satisfy the needs of the oppressed, then your light will rise in the darkness, and your night will become like the noonday. The Lord will guide you always; He will satisfy your needs in a sun-scorched land and will strengthen your frame. You will be like a well-watered garden, like a spring whose waters never fail (NIV).

What an amazing picture of God's protection and provision when we obey His commands to take care of the needy! That is what I want from God—that He would continually guide me, that He would give strength to my bones so I can do His will, that I would be like a beautiful watered garden that blooms and draws people to the Creator. If taking care of the poor because it's God's command isn't enough, that promise certainly motivates me! The strange irony that happens when we serve others is that our own healing often comes in the process. *Not because we go looking for the reward,* rather His love for me motivates me to put aside my own needs and to share His concerns for the lost, poor and needy. The Holy Spirit works through our obedience and everyone benefits.

PERSONAL REFLECTION: Caring for others in compassionate service can be demanding, tiring and profoundly healing. Spend some time contemplating specific passages in Scripture such as Isaiah 58, Mathew 25 and 1 Timothy 6:17-19.

How can you respond to those in need around you? Ask God to guide you and your community in creative ways to work for justice and mercy.

CHAPTER 9

Sharing our Faith

I suppose the first thing we must do is to recapture what the Gospel truly is. We had a death sentence hanging over our heads because of sin. Jesus, the lamb slain from the foundation of the world, has rescued (saved) us by His death. His resurrection opened the doors of heaven for us. We are the prodigal, and the Father has run to us to welcome us home. That is the Gospel. We need to share it.

- Jeff Dunn[15]

O ur faith is founded on Christ. It's founded on the fact that Jesus is God, in a real person, whose purpose in life was to reconcile us to Himself. He came so that we may have life and have it abundantly (John 10:10 NKJV).

That is a rich truth that I want everyone to know. I want them to know a life of freedom in Christ, of communion with

---

[15] Jeff Dunn. Internet Monk. *Saving Evangelicalism, Part Two.* January 17th 2013

119

God, of transformation. Witnessing, or sharing with others what God has done in your life, is a part of being a Christian. We are called to bear witness to that truth, freedom and communion, to offer others the hope of the Gospel.

What does that mean at work?

Are We Supposed to be an Evangelist in Our Field?

As we discussed earlier, there's a school of thought that says that Christians are to interact with the world for the exclusive purpose of sharing the gospel. In their book, *Your Work Matters to God,* Sherman and Hendricks refer to that approach as the "Strategic Soapbox" model. They write that, "Christians should work in secular jobs primarily as a strategy for evangelism. If you adopt this Strategic Soapbox model for your life, you redefine your job description. You are no longer a doctor, a teacher, or a salesperson. Rather, you become an evangelist in the field of medicine, education, or marketing."

Just after they identify the model, they discredit it: "Your work matters to God. Work is not something beneath God's dignity or concern, as some contend. Nor is work a game we play with non-Christians in order to accomplish a more important agenda. Work is a major part of human life that God takes seriously." If we think that our only purpose for being in a profession is to share the gospel with that group of people, are we giving the right amount of energy to our actual jobs? Put another way, does neglecting our job glorify God?

I think it's the "Strategic Soapbox" model that ruins a lot of opportunities. Sometimes our "sharing" is a sermon in disguise. Taking the word at its literal definition, "witness" means to testify, just like a witness in court, to our firsthand, personal experience about what God has done in our lives. It's not about preaching, but rather, "Just the facts, ma'am." Sometimes, though, we aren't sharing "just the facts" about what God has done in our lives. We are offering "just our opinion" about what other people should do differently in their lives. When our conversation comes from a place of trying to convince others, it makes people suspicious of our motives and message.

We also need to realize that in some workplaces, we may be strictly prohibited from sharing our faith because of human resources policies. I heard of a 62-year old woman, I'll call Sarah, who had worked for the same OB/GYN clinic for 30 years. Over that time, she decorated her cubicle for each of the holidays: Thanksgiving, Christmas, Easter, Independence Day. For 29 years, that had been the accepted norm—until she received a written warning from the clinic's new Human Resources manager. She was informed that celebrating holidays was an outward reflection of her faith (crosses, Christmas decorations, etc.) and could lead to her immediate termination. Knowing that the economy was tough and jobs for 62-year-olds were hard to find, Sarah accepted the terms of the human resources letter and no longer shows any outward signs of her faith.

Is Evangelism *Part* of the Purpose for Working?

If one of our purposes for working is coming into contact with the world to show God's love through our professional and personal actions by doing important work well, then yes— hopefully evangelism will be a natural outflow of your work at some time.

We talked about how *not* to share: that our job is not a strategic soapbox, that we shouldn't camouflage a sermon as sharing, or violate our employer's policy. Yet God does call us to "go into all the world and make disciples." People need to hear about Christ before they start living like Him, so when exactly is it appropriate to discuss our faith and how do we do it?

As we prepare to talk to someone about Jesus we need to ask ourselves who we are really thinking of when we share the truth of Christ. Are we doing it because we really care about this person and God created the opportunity for a conversation? Or are we talking to them about Jesus because we know we are "supposed to" share our faith and forcing a conversation that wouldn't naturally occur? Don't get me wrong; God can still use those conversations, but I think it is important that we know our own motives.

When we explain the gospel to someone out of some sense of obligation, to "check the box" that we've told someone about Jesus, we are primarily doing it for our own benefit. A lot of evangelism training starts that way: we approach strangers because it isn't as intimidating as discussing what you believe with someone you know. Training like that was invaluable as I learned how to articulate the gospel clearly. But we need to make the transition into talking about the Good News of Jesus with people we love because we deeply care for them, not because we feel obligated or guilty or see it as "practice" in the same way a salesman might need to practice his pitch.

Although there are many examples of people coming to know Christ through a stranger, most people learn about Jesus from someone who cares about them and with whom they've established a personal relationship, like a parent, a teacher, a friend, a college roommate, a supportive colleague, or another parent on the playground.

Some Things to Keep in Mind:

Know yourself: A friend of mine is a teacher. As we were talking about this issue, she told me of the way people's own personalities were evident in their approach to the teachers' lounge. One Christian colleague of hers never enters the teachers' lounge, choosing instead to stay in her classroom during lunch every day and during her breaks. To her, the conversations are uncomfortable and unhealthy. Another of my friend's Christian colleagues seemed to find a door open to talk about Jesus in every conversation.

My friend said she was somewhere in the middle. She goes to the teacher's lounge and engages with her colleagues, but she doesn't feel comfortable bringing up Jesus' name all the time.

We all know those people who just seem to ooze Jesus. A conversation between them and the cashier at the grocery store turns into the cashier crying and sharing his life story and coming to church the next weekend. But if that isn't who we are, we don't need to force it. Instead, we need to allow our own strengths and personality traits to express our faith in natural, organic ways. And we need to be available to our colleagues should they ask questions.

Know Your Audience: When we want to make a compelling presentation to anyone from our bosses to the zoning committee, we must know our audience. We need to know who we are talking to, what their current perspective is, what their preferences are. How well do we know our colleagues? Do we know what their perspectives on faith and life are? Are we curious about them?

When I was thinking about this chapter, I decided to take my own advice and I asked some non-Christian friends to share their experiences when Christians have discussed their faith with them. Several of the things I'm covering here are points they made. If we're honest about how we feel with someone approaching us about something important, these points make a lot of sense.

Understand different environments: I was talking with a former Marine friend whose father was also in the military when he was growing up. He spoke of the "instant familiarity" that he had with other military families. They may not be from the same place, but they can be pretty sure that they have similar experiences and values. They become good friends fast. However, he had to learn how to have relationships with civilians because they didn't always want to get to know him that quickly. He realized he couldn't make the same assumptions about them that he could usually make about other service members.

I think one can draw a parallel here between the military community and the Christian community. When we meet another Christian, we usually make assumptions about them (beyond just stereotypes) of their experiences, doctrine, etc. A lot of Christians are used to "speaking the same language" when they meet people at Bible study and immediately share their personal struggles. Should we expect our co-workers to have this instant desire to share their lives with us? Outside a given community—military or Christian—it takes time and effort to become a trusted friend.

To many of us, our faith is an integral part of our lives. We are open about who Christ is and what He has done for us. But to many others, faith can be a very private topic. Walking into our work place wearing a bumper sticker with our faith on it (or any other "touchy issue" for that matter) will probably be met with mixed reactions. Part of knowing our audience is realizing when it's okay to discuss personal topics.

Build a Relationship: My non-Christian friends also told me that when someone cares about them and expresses their concern, it's meaningful. If someone who has no relationship with them tries to tell them how to live their lives or what choices to make, it's a big turnoff. Getting to know a colleague over time and living alongside them can give us a deep concern for them and create a place of influence in their lives, just like they will have in ours. The more time we spend together, the more we can talk to them about important, personal issues from a place of mutual respect and trust.

My friends said they were more likely to be responsive if the Christian had developed a genuine relationship with them. A stranger can convince us that some new beer or make-up product will make us cooler. But when it comes to the deep issues of life, it's not usually a stranger who makes the impact. It's someone who knows us and loves us, someone who has our best interests at heart—not their bottom line. So sharing something as important as the gospel with anyone—colleague or family member—should come from a place of deep care for the other person.

Know the Time and Place: If we do feel led to share the gospel verbally, it might be helpful to know how to discern the appropriate time and place. One of my friends told me she didn't mind anyone sharing things that were important to them if it was part of a natural dialogue. According to her, there's a right time and a right place. The right place for it is not at work. Work is not a place to flirt or to have a book club; it's also not the place for unsolicited conversations about faith. She goes to work to work and expects her colleagues to do the same.

The right time is likely not in the middle of the workday. There may be rare occasions when we are behind closed doors with a colleague and she is confiding about a problem. But that would likely only happen after we had built a relationship with her and spent more time with her outside of work. When cube walls and deadlines don't surround us, there will be more freedom for conversation.

How do we let them know that our interest is motivated by Christ's love? That's a tough one. One friend said that when people write, "I'm praying for you" in a sympathy card, she finds it a bit off-putting. And if they add anything else to it, such as, "Praying that Christ will comfort you," she gets offended. She said, "If you believe prayer works, just pray and keep it to yourself. Why do you have to tell me?"

As Christians we are called to *bear one another's burdens and thus fulfill the laws of Christ* (Galatians 6:2, NKJV). When friends carry burdens for me by praying for me—sometimes I can physically feel the weight lifting. But this doesn't translate to my friend. She doesn't see it as carrying a burden with her; she sees it as a bit presumptuous.

I'm not saying we can never sign a card, "I'm praying for you." At times, that could be just what is appropriate and necessary. The point is that we check to see if our default response always brings our faith into the conversation. Or is our default response to check what we know about our audience? We want to take these opportunities to pull people close to us, not push them away, and thinking of ways we can be supportive in practical, helpful, ways signals our compassion.

Just Love Them: As we serve others, though, we must keep checking our motives. Why are we showing love to them? Is it because we actually love them? Is it because we want to show God's love to them? We need to differentiate between an opportunity to share our faith and an opportunity just to love someone else, with no other agenda. It is disingenuous to share our faith but not to love, or to share our faith in place of love.

People are not projects. Our love for them should not be driven by some hidden agenda of one desired outcome. Our job is to step lovingly into the lives of our colleagues and care for them. Even if we never see the "result" of a new faith, God calls us to love others as He has loved us.

Let Them Find the Answers: I know of a couple who recently went for marriage counseling. In the first session, the counselor listened to them for about half an hour, and then spent the rest of their session telling them what they were doing wrong. The counselor may have been right in her assessments but the couple didn't care. They hadn't gone to a counselor to be told all the answers. They'd gone to a counselor for a "discovery experience." They already had an idea of what they weren't getting right, but they wanted to have a chance to figure it out.

Who can't remember being a teenager and discovering something our parents had been trying to tell us for years? When we fail to invite people into the process, we remove the chance for them to figure it out for themselves. We remove the ownership that they would feel over their decision had they come to the conclusion themselves. This is especially true when it comes to something incredibly personal—a person's faith.

Loving in the midst of value differences

As we build relationships with colleagues and establish an authentic sense of trust and support, they begin to understand that we want to love them not judge them. Many times over the years I've heard pastors or church leaders say that, "Jesus hung out with prostitutes and tax collectors—we should, too."

How I wish I knew what Jesus talked about with them! Did He ask them how business was going? Did He listen patiently when they joked about ripping off taxpayers?

I wonder, because sometimes I don't know how to, or am afraid to, have conversations with people whose values differ from mine. Recently a good friend told me she feels constrained by monogamy and is exploring what she describes as *ethical non-monogamy* (more than one partner, where all partners are aware of each other). She shared this with me because we have cultivated strong trust and she wanted to honor our friendship by showing her authentic self to me. She'd been afraid to tell me because she knew that I value monogamy and feared I would judge her rather than simply value her disclosure. She also feared that since I am in a monogamous marriage her disclosure might come across as judging me, which was not her intention.

The day she told me I could tell we were having a precious conversation. My goal was to be loving towards my friend in the tension of our diverging values. And that is my ongoing goal; as she tries to be loving towards me. But we still both have to be ourselves, as complicated as that can be. We continue to talk about our romantic lives, as I do with all my close friends. We've had a chance to ask each other question about our choices and viewpoints, we've both been refined as a result if those conversations.

After all, one of the more crucial moments in a relationship is when someone reveals an intimate secret that doesn't align with our values. How do we react to that revelation? Are we horrified or confused or judgmental through our words or body language, or do we have questions at the ready so we can digest the news? How can we honor the relationship and convey love at the same time being open about where a values difference exists?

I've found this might take at least two conversations: the first focused on listening and a second—if they are willing—on exploring. I've found a few responses or questions have been helpful in these situations:

- Thank you for sharing that with me; I'm not sure if it was difficult given perceived differences in our values. I want to reassure you that I am interested in knowing about your life.
- Tell me more.
- What has led you to this decision?
- What have you learned so far?
- How are you handling XYZ?

- What do your family and other close friends think?
- Acknowledging that we may have different values on this, what can I do to support you?

If my friend was a Christian and we had a close relationship, I would have followed what it says in Galatians 6:1-2: "Brothers and sisters, if someone is caught in a sin, you who live by the Spirit should restore that person gently. But watch yourselves, or you also may be tempted." I would have gently talked to her about her decisions and about how they don't line up with the picture the Bible gives for intimate relationships. I would have wanted to help her restore her faith in God's design.

But she's not a Christian. And while she values my opinion, she isn't trying to live her life by the same values I do. So what is the Christ-like thing to do in this situation? How would Jesus ask her about her different partners? How would He show concern and love for her without showing endorsement of those decisions or condemnation of her as a person? As the Savior and Messiah, Jesus could and did tell people to go and sin no more. But when the religious people started calling out the sins of others, Jesus said, *Let anyone of you who is without sin be the first to throw a stone at her.* (John 8:7, NIV)

So how do I express biblical values without throwing stones? Or is it even my place to express these values if she's not asking for my opinion? What is my role in this situation?

It's important to express genuine interest in your colleagues, including those from diverse religions or no religion at all as well as those who are in different romantic arrangements, and those who reside in different spots along the political spectrum.

It can be difficult to know how to engage in these situations, and my fear is that we will disengage when it gets tough. Will we pull ourselves inward, and retreat to our "safe" Christian bubbles where we don't have to encounter the rest of the world? But if we do that, where will people learn about the love Christ has for them? If we aren't "out there," what are the chances of them coming "in here"?

I'm not applauding my "compassion," or my open mindedness. There is no "us," and there is no "them." I know that I am sinful, and I know that my friend bears the image of God. But I don't want to minimize the fact that when values diverge, this tension is hard to navigate.

In his book, *Roaring Lambs*, Bob Briner wrote, "There are times when God calls us to speak out against evil—we are called to defend widows and orphans. But I don't think it's our job to perpetually criticize people and institutions for their failings. It's our job to build better people and better institutions." We need to build people up and encourage them towards excellence a lot more often than we need to pull them down for decisions we disagree with.

Remember That It's a Process

We live in a results-oriented culture: tell me about last quarter's numbers; how many pounds you have lost; how many countries you have visited. Not only do we expect visible results, we expect them *immediately*. Too often our Christian world keeps track this way, too: church growth often refers to a rising number of attendees, we feel like the small group we're leading is a failure when only two people show up, or we count how many people we've talked about Jesus with to see if we're doing "enough."

Sure, it's great to see results of hard work in the form of higher profits or lower weight. And it's wonderful when more people are drawn into church and presented with the opportunity to grow closer to God. But when we approach "sharing our faith" with the goal of a particular result—we're in trouble. The importance of prayerfully approaching conversations of faith cannot be understated. Mark Batterson's book—*The Circle Maker*—provides guidance for using prayer to allow God to accomplish His agenda through us, not just pushing our own will. Trust Him for the hearts of people in your life, not your own efforts.

Recently I was spending time with a casual acquaintance. She asked me about my spiritual practices. I got tongue-tied. Here was my chance! I wanted to tell her how fabulous Christ is, but what if I screwed it up? So, I got a little overly excited, explaining way too much. I had an agenda—I wanted to convince her that Christ is the way, the truth and the life (John 14:6). What I should have done was shared my experience with her, and then asked her about her spiritual practices.

It's a good thing that Scripture doesn't tell us that we'll be able to overcome the world by the power of our ability to convince others! It tells us instead that we will overcome the world by the power of our testimony (Revelation 12:11). I've heard it described as "the difference between a car-salesman and a satisfied customer." When we go into a car dealership, we know we're being *sold* to. But when I encounter someone who loves her car, it feels different; she just shares her experience of her car. She isn't concerned what her personal gains might be from telling me about the car; she's just telling me what she knows and loves. And in some ways she can't help it; love compels her.

Paul uses agricultural images to show the process of someone's faith growing. There's a lot to be done—and without good preparation, we can't expect to grow much. Different people perform different tasks: someone who does the planting may not be the same person who does the watering. And we may never be there to see the harvesting. As Paul wrote in 1 Corinthians 3:5-9, *The Lord gave opportunity to each one. I planted, Apollos watered, but God was causing the growth. So then neither the one who plants nor the one who waters is anything, but God who causes the growth.* (NASB).

Our job is to remember that we could be playing any number of roles in someone's faith journey (planter, tender, water-er, harvester), but we probably aren't playing all those roles at the same time. So we can remove any pressure we might feel that it's our job to convince someone, and that it's up to us to "close the deal" before she walks out the door.

A friend, I'll call him James, recounted a story of his time in the Army. His former first sergeant was pretty tough on him and his Christian buddy. Things the sergeant had said led James to think it was because of their faith. A few years later, the sergeant called James. He'd recently had surgery, and for the first time he felt "mortal." He respected James's faith after their time together in Iraq and wanted his opinion on where to look for spiritual direction. James then explained the gospel to the sergeant. But it turns out that James wasn't the only one who had planted seeds: the sergeant told James, "Oh, so that's what Bill was talking about!" It took the influence of many people and a stretch of time for my friend to have an open door to talk with the sergeant about his faith.

But in God's timing, he had the opportunity because it grew out of an authentic relationship.

PERSONAL REFLECTION: Only God can transform someone's soul. We are invited to work alongside Him. Prepare the soil of your workplace through prayer: pray for your work environment, pray for your colleagues, pray for what's going on in their lives, pray for God's leading for how best to love them, and pray for natural opportunities to share Christ with them. Go to where your colleagues are and be present in their lives.

"As God awakens man to faith by His Holy Spirit,
He Himself posits the necessary point of contact."
– Karl Barth

CHAPTER 10

Figuring Out Where We Fit In

Not long ago, I was out for drinks with some colleagues. Fun conversations were raging all around me and I just couldn't seem to break in. I didn't know enough about the topics people were talking about to participate and I was at a loss to come up with new subjects. I was watching other people have a good time and wondered to myself why I was even there. I just didn't fit in.

I've had those moments at church, too. When I'm committed to completing an important project for work over the next few weekends and I have to miss the church retreat, I sometimes get the impression that my fellow church-goers think I'm not as spiritually committed as they are. It sometimes seems that the people who take on the most church responsibilities are viewed as the most spiritual—and no one wants to seem like a slacker at church!

Conversations with other working women tell me they feel a similar tension of never quite belonging in one place or another.

We Are Not Alone

We may feel out of place at work or at church, or both. But are professional women the only ones who feel like we don't fit in? Absolutely not.

A friend of mine recently got divorced and said he feels so out of place at church, he wonders if he should even keep attending. Another friend was a refugee from a country in Asia. She'd seen so much pain in her life she had a hard time relating to people who had grown up amidst peace and seemed uncaring about the injustices in other parts of the world.

A woman at my former church had a chronic illness and felt like she'd worn out her welcome by asking for help. No one remembered to visit her. And a missionary I supported has been open about feeling like people send financial support without investing emotionally.

Friends who have been laid off from work want to give up on going to social events because they are tired of the dreaded "so what do you do?" question, as if that's the only thing that defines them.

The examples continue. A gentleman at my church has a mental illness and feels like he can't make real friends there, just "sympathy" friends. A woman took an unpaid internship because that was all she could find after graduating. Three very recent college graduates are working full time at the same company where she's interning. She has a hard time feeling like a peer in the break room.

And several friends from church who are facing infertility tell me how overwhelmed they feel with all the strollers and baby carriers every Sunday and wonder what their biblical perspective should be. At the same time, young mothers think the church could provide a better support system for new families who no longer live near their extended families. And some friends don't have a desire to have children and feel like they have to defend themselves in a family-centric society.

Junior high students—need I say more?

We have all struggled to belong.

The long list of needs around us can feel overwhelming, but it can also give us perspective. It is part of the human condition to feel like we just don't quite fit in. That's not an excuse; it is the reality of living in this imperfect and broken world. It's not just us as professional women who can feel out of place. Honestly, I can't think of a single person I know who feels like she or he completely and totally belongs. Some people may just be better at faking it!

We're not supposed to belong.

Let me return to that outing with work friends that I shared at the beginning of this chapter. I was sitting there thinking about how I didn't fit in with them and feeling outside the conversation. I really wanted to belong, but I just didn't. I said to myself, "I don't belong here." At the same time, I felt God's still, small voice say to my spirit, "You aren't supposed to."

I don't think that God was saying, "Eh, don't worry about it. Don't try to learn new things or make new friends." I think we should engage with the world around us and seek to contribute to our jobs, our relationships, our society.

What I think God was saying that night to me was along the lines of when the great British thinker C.S. Lewis wrote, "If we find ourselves with a desire that nothing in this world can satisfy, the most probable explanation is that we were made for another world."

We're citizens of another Kingdom. A Kingdom that is coming. But a Kingdom that isn't here yet. I'm not supposed to feel perfectly comfortable here on earth because I was made for heaven. Until Jesus returns we have to sit through awkward conversations where we feel like we can't connect. Some people in different parts of the world literally have to worship in private because it's illegal for them to worship in the open. Others have to face war outside their front door because broken people are running their country's political systems.

So it's okay that as professional Christian women we feel like we don't quite belong either in work-circles, where people focus on different things, or in church circles, where many of the women are stay-at-home moms.

It may seem like a big leap to go from "not being able to make small talk" to "it's a reflection of God-given hunger for heaven." But all those times we feel out of place, or like we don't connect, can remind us that we're not just waiting for Jesus to return. We've been given the extraordinary privilege of helping to bring God's Kingdom here to Earth, just as Jesus said in the Lord's prayer, "Your kingdom come, Your will be done on Earth as it is in Heaven." We're called to create just economic systems and to fight for righteousness. We're instructed to make a difference for the poor and marginalized. We're invited to engage with the world around us and make it more peaceful and just for everyone.

Dutch politician and theologian, Abraham Kuyper, was a powerful voice to people seeking to connect their faith with the rest of their lives. He is well known for having said: "No single piece of our mental world is to be hermetically sealed off from the rest, and there is not a square inch in the whole domain of our human existence over which Christ, who is Sovereign over all, does not cry: 'Mine!'"[16] Normally only the second half of that quote is used, and it is certainly encouraging as we seek to influence our society for good. As we try to make better schoolrooms and boardrooms, city governments, churches and laboratories, Kuyper reminds us that Christ cares about every single inch of our existence.

But the first part of the quote is encouraging to me as well, in those moments when I am locked inside my brain, worried how I don't fit in, worried that I will never make a difference, worried too much about what other people think. All of our mental world is under Christ's domain as well. So we can step forward with confidence to use the gifts and skills He has given us to serve others. When, with Christ's presence, we can overcome some of those mental acrobatics, then we can move outside ourselves and help bring about real change in the places we work, the communities we live and the world God loves.

The Church's Job

The problem is when we think it's the "Church's" job to solve our problems of not fitting in, and all these other problems. Especially when we think the church is either that brick-and-mortar building we show up to on weekends or the people who make up the leadership of that congregation. Are only those

---

[16] 1880 Inaugural Lecture, Free University of Amsterdam; Kuyper, Abraham (1998). "Sphere Sovereignty". In Bratt, James D.. Abraham Kuyper, A Centennial Reader. Grand Rapids, MI: Eerdmans. page. 488

people who work in that building responsible for creating a meal rotation for families with new babies? Should they alone be in charge of creating an employment ministry for the unemployed? Are they the only ones qualified to start a support group for people who have gone through divorce?

There are so many ways the church could improve, but we tend to employ filters that highlight how the church is ignoring *our specific need*. Lots of needs go unmet, and lots of people feel like the church doesn't understand them.

But the reality of the Gospel is that the Church is *us*. It's our job to meet the needs of those who are hurting around us. As individuals, we often feel ill-equipped to speak into the unique aspects of someone else's life and minister directly to something we know nothing about. But if Christ's promises are true, we don't need to feel ill-equipped. God Himself equips us! He gives us the words to soothe someone's hurts, or the money to meet someone else's need. He's the one who moves us to compassion.

And often He leads us in ways we never imagined He would. For instance, I love my church's small group system. My church believes that discipleship can happen anywhere, so our leadership encourages people to start a small group around a personal passion. That's where I got the idea to start a small group for professional Christian women. I felt like women's Bible studies I'd attended weren't helping me figure out how to integrate my faith with my work, which was really important to me. So I started a Bible study on the topic. My church gave me permission to come up with a solution to a problem I saw.

There are also small groups for people who've gone through divorces so they can identify with one another and help each other recover. That's why there are moms' clubs and singles ministries.

Oftentimes authentic friendships are built between people who have shared experiences and struggles. And when we're more connected and more healed, we can reach out and give to others who are experiencing a different type of distance from the church than our own. If we say we aren't equipped to help others, we're ignoring 2 Timothy 3:16-17, which says we are *thoroughly equipped for every good work*. By way of God's Scripture, He gives us the teaching and the training to help others. I may not understand everything a single mom is going through, but I can listen with empathy, offer to help her, and point her towards other mothers who have the experience I lack.

Identity in Christ

Whether we feel like we don't fit in at work or at church, we need to give ourselves constant reminders that our identity is in Christ. The reality of who we are, is anchored in what God says about us in the Word. We *are*:

- Accepted (Ephesians 1:6 NKJV)
- Co-heirs with Christ (Romans 8:17)
- Redeemed and forgiven (Colossians 1:14)
- Chosen to bear fruit (John 15:16)
- One of God's living stones, being built into a spiritual house (1 Peter 2:5)

Our identity then is not in whatever role we happen to be filling in a given hour, day or year. As important as those roles are, the roles are not all that define us. Instead, we can persevere knowing that we are honoring God with our unique skills in the workplace, that the Creator of the Universe is with us wherever He leads us and we "fit in" with Him.

PERSONAL REFLECTION: We may not fit in to a particular environment—a predominantly male workplace, a "success at all costs" office, a busy church, or a society that doesn't have a Christian worldview. We're all misfits, really. But we DO fit in to God's family. We belong to God. We are the Body of Christ, the Church. And as the Church, it's our job to make sure other people know they fit in as well.

Keep an eye out in the next few days for someone who needs to be reminded that they fit in to God's family. Let your encouragement of them serve to remind you that you fit in as well.

CONCLUSION

My hopes for you
as a professional Christian woman

I hope you've learned some powerful truths about God and yourself.

I hope you were able to "get grounded"—to learn what the Bible says about contributing to our society through work, to move forward on tough issues like determining your calling or maintaining work/life balance.

I hope you were able to "get real" with yourself, and maybe some friends, about the struggles we face as professional Christian women—struggles to be confident of our contributions, struggles to have healthy relationships with the men we work with, and struggles to live above reproach. I hope you know you aren't alone in those challenges.

And I hope this book has motivated you to "get going" to feel comfortable integrating your work and your faith; to realize that whatever your role you belong in the Body of Christ. I hope you are also motivated to identify opportunities to build up that Body.

Now here's a vision of what we can do together: I challenge you, woman of God, to be confident in your identity in Christ and in your calling to follow Him. I challenge you to confront the needs of this world with the skills God has given you, to not be afraid to serve Him wherever he calls you.

AFTERWORD

By Diane Paddison

We created 4word—an organization dedicated to professional Christian women—because the demographics of the professional world are shifting:

- In 2010, over 50% of advanced degrees went to women, compared to the 1970s when only 10% of advanced degrees went to women
- As of 2010, women are the primary breadwinners in 40% of families; compared to just 6% in 1976
- As of 2008, in two-income households, 26% of women earn more than their spouse, compared to 16% in 1985[17]

These shifts have far-reaching implications. The proportion of young women viewing their jobs in the context of a long-term career path with significant financial implications for both them and their families has exploded. These women are hungry for mentors and colleagues who have navigated the path ahead of them to provide them with leadership and

---

[17] Data Compiled from US Census Bureau report entitled "Women in the Workforce;" Bureau of Labor Statistics "Overview of BLS Statistics on Women Workers" and statistical analysis performed by Catalyst

impart wisdom as they make their way through the professional world and their families.

This is particularly true for Christian women who often feel that they have an additional dynamic—their faith— to assimilate: the modern workplace often represents the environment with the greatest separation from God.

Although there are exceptions, most professional environments are perceived to present more challenges to one's faith than opportunities to grow in it. Forces of evil have somehow successfully carved out the workplace as the inappropriate venue for God. As a response, the majority of Christians adopt some degree of a "compartmentalized" approach between their faith and work. As work occupies an ever-increasing percentage of professional Christian women's time and energy, this creates a significant risk of progressive "faith drift."

Sadly, many professional women are finding the traditional church lacking in bringing them closer to God. In 2011, 84% of Christian 18- to 29-year-olds acknowledged they had no idea how the Bible applies to their field or professional interests.[18] Could that be part of the reason why 'millennials' and professional Christian women are leaving the church? Part of this exodus reflects broader cultural trends but some of it relates to relevancy and shared values for professional Christian women, including the issue of women prioritizing working inside or outside the home.

Because of these trends, professional Christian women need content, community and mentors to help them assimilate the priorities of work, relationships and family, and faith (or

---

[18] Barna Research Group. Top Trends of 2011, December 2011

Work, Love, Pray as my book is entitled and how we structure our efforts at 4word). Without focus and intentionality, the most pressing of these three activities on a daily basis (work or family) usually gets an elevated status and it leads to neglect or subordination of the most significant but also most "off-puttable" (God/prayer) of these and leads to negative consequences in all aspects of life.

In *Faith Powered Profession,* Elizabeth provides a resource to meet this growing need. She is thoughtful to integrate biblical values and the challenges of everyday life. Her insights are both philosophical and practical. Her book is a portable mentor for professional Christian women who are seeking to understand the importance of their work, know how to approach the challenges we face there, and ensure that we live our lives holistically—without separating our faith from the rest of our lives.

I am proud to be a part of a growing movement of professional Christian women seeking to know God and make Him known, while serving Him in the professional world. I am grateful for Elizabeth's commitment to that same movement.

Diane Paddison
Founder of 4word, www.4wordwomen.org
Author of *Work, Love, Pray*
Chief Strategy Officer of Cassidy Turley
Former Executive Team member of two
Fortune 500 companies, CBRE and ProLogis

STUDY GUIDE

Chapter 1
What We Are Doing is Important

1. Where do Christians "belong?"
   - Do you feel like you "should" be in full-time ministry to be a "good Christian?"
   - Do Christians belong in the business/professional world?
     + What Scripture would you use to support either view?
     + What would you say to someone who does think that full-time ministry is the best way for Christians to serve God?
   - Do you believe that some jobs are holier than others?
     + What kind of jobs are holy?
     + What kind of jobs aren't holy?

2. Read Matthew 5:13-14
   - How does working in a professional environment allow us to fulfill God's commands "to be the salt and light" and "to be in the world, not of the world?"
   - How are you salt and light to the world around you?
   - How do you come in contact with the world and try to preserve it, to make it more flavorful?

3. Read John 17:6-19
   - Do you feel comfortable being fully engaged in the world around you?

4. Work as Worship
   - Can you see what gifts God has given you that you can give back to Him as an act of worship?

5. Your Work is Important
   - Is being "salt-and-light" the only reason we're called to professional occupations?
   - How does the work itself matter?
   - How should we perform that work?
   - How are you seeking the peace and prosperity of the city to which God has called you?

Chapter 2
Where Does a Christian Women Belong?

1. Why are we asking the question: "Where does a Christian woman belong?"

2. What is your experience with the Church's expectations of women?
   - Do you feel implicit or explicit pressure to meet certain expectations? Do you think the expectations are Biblical or cultural?
   - Have you ever felt like the young woman at the beginning of the chapter, wondering if you are "less of a Christian woman" if you make different choices from the typical Christian woman?

3. What Scripture do you use to inform your perspective on God's call on your life as a woman? As a professional woman?

4. What is your understanding of the complementarian and egalitarian perspectives? Do you identify with one side more than the other?

5. How can you be a part of building mutual respect about the variety of ways God calls women to serve Him?

Chapter 3
Finding Our Work/Life Balance

1. What do you think when you hear "Work/Life Balance?"
   - Work is bad, life is good…or is it?
   - Read Colossians 3:23-24

2. How do YOU decide if your work/life balance is working out?
   - What behaviors does work influence in you? Does it energize you? Drain you?
   - How do you feel when you interact with others? Happy? Exhausted? Cheerful? Crabby?
   - Other questions to ask yourself?

3. Is "balance" an achievable, steady state?
   - What are the "big rocks" for you in this season of life?
   - Does the way you're spending your time reflect your priorities?

4. Whether we have perfect balance or not, the Bible addresses the Importance of Rest. What is the main point of each of these verses?
   - Genesis 2:2
   - Exodus 20:11
   - Exodus 31:13
   - Colossians 2:16
   - Hebrews 4:4

- Why did God create the Sabbath?
- Even though we are no longer under the law, why is this important?
- When was the last time you observed a Sabbath day?
- What kind of boundaries can you set in your life to make rest and the Sabbath a priority?

5. Besides rest, what are other things we need to make priorities in our schedules?
- Hebrews 4:12
- 1 Corinthians 6:19-20
- Others

Chapter 4

Determining Our Calling

1. What are the general callings of God?
- 1 John 4:19
- Luke 10:27
- James 1:27
- Others

2. When you hear "determine" or "discover" you're calling, what do you think?
  - your job
  - your geographic location
  - others
- Why do we tend to think of our vocational calling as our whole calling? What are some of the dangers of thinking your job is your whole calling?

3. Imagine you are presented with two different job offers? How do you discern between the two of them? Could you possibly choose the wrong one?
- Hebrews 5:14

4. Chapter 3 listed several things your calling may not be: instant, risk free, etc.
- What else is it not?

"The place God calls you to is where your deep gladness and the world's deep hunger meet."
— Frederick Buechner,
in his book *Wishful Thinking*

Chapter 5
The Only One in the Room

1. What thoughts/emotions does the phrase "gender equality" bring up in you?

2. How do the following verses inform your ideas of gender roles?
- Genesis 1:26-27
- Genesis 3 (pay attention to verse 16)
- Galatians 3:26-28
- Acts 10:34-35
- What other verses influence your perspective on gender relationships?

3. How has gender been a factor in how you approach the following issues? How do the verses above impact your perspective on these issues?
- Discrimination
- Leadership Opportunities
- Unwanted Attention
- Sexual Harassment

"We have equal rights because we have the same Creator. Both the dignity and the equality of human beings are traced in Scripture to our creation. This principle should be even more obvious to the New Testament community, since we have the same Saviour also."

John Stott,
Involvement: Being a Responsible Christian in a Non-Christian Society, p. 200

Chapter 6
The Men We Work With

1. What types of interactions do you have with your male colleagues?
   - Do any of your interactions border on the inappropriate?
   - Are any of them flat-out over the line?

2. Read:
   - Matthew 5:28-29
   - Matthew 12:35
   - Matthew 18:7
   - Hebrews 13:5
   - 1 John 1:12

3. With those verses as Biblical context, how do we approach the following?
   - "Harmless Flirting"
   - Filling a Void
     - Acceptance
     - Security
     - Identity
   - Emotional Affairs
   - Physical Affairs

4. What are some "gateway behaviors" you see in your own life right now? Things you are doing that could open the door to unhealthy relationships with the men you work with?

5. Have you encountered consequences of making poor decisions in this area?

6. What examples do you have of healthy male/female relationships—in your own life or in the lives of others?

Chapter 7
Why Morals Matter

1. What does "Living Above Reproach" mean to you?
   - 1 Timothy 3:1-7
   - Does this apply to you if you're not an elder?
   - What does apply to you about living a "moral life?"

2. What can little mistakes do to our voice to speak into people's lives?

3. How do you stop yourself from getting legalistic and more concerned with rules than with your heart?

4. Name two things—big or little—you need to "check in on."
   - What are you going to do about them?
   - Is there anyone you need to approach for forgiveness?

5. What are some ways you can make better decisions?
   - Encouragement/Guidance from Scripture
     - Joshua 24:15
     - 1 Timothy 4:16
     - 1 Peter 1:15-16
     - Ephesians 4:20-24
   - Decide about your behavior early on
   - Have an accountability partner
   - Others

The question is, who wasn't messy? Noah the drunk, Moses the murderer, David the adulterer, Eli the screwed up priest, Samson the lustful hunk. The disciples were not exactly models of discipleship, or should I say they were models of real discipleship. Trouble is, over the centuries we've tried to make them something they weren't. The real disciples were inconsistent, erratic, confused, frustrated, afraid, full of doubt. More often than not they didn't understand a word Jesus was saying. That's very encouraging, by the way, because if what I just described is real discipleship, then I can be one.

Mike Yaconelli

Chapter 8
A "For-Benefit" Life

1. What do the following verses call us to?
   - James 2:26
   - Matthew 20:25-28
   - John 13:2-5

2. Do you feel like you're living as a servant?
   - Does your job help you serve others, or do you feel like it's a hindrance to serving others?

3. Who are the poor around you? How are they in need?

4. How could you envision a more holistic life of service?
   - What are the various ways to give?
     - Time
     - Skills
     - Tithing/Offering
     - Others

5. Read Isaiah 58:10-12
   - How does that verse inspire you?

Chapter 9
Sharing our Faith

1. How do you feel about sharing your faith in general?
   - What do you think of when you think about "sharing your faith" in a work environment?
   - Are we called to be "evangelists" in our field?
   - How and when is it appropriate?
   - How and when is it inappropriate?
   - Is sharing your faith the main purpose of you being at work?

2. Read Acts 17:16-34
   - As the apostle Paul walked through Athens, what did he see? Why do you think the things he saw troubled him so deeply?
   - Why did Paul get the opportunity to speak to the Athenians? What made him relevant?
   - If you were in the audience when Paul spoke, what would keep your attention?
   - What were the three responses to Paul's presentation?

3. Know your audience/establishing commonality
   - Jot down 5 things you have in common with your co-workers:
     -
     -
     -
     -
     -

4. Where are you planting seeds right now? Watering? Cultivating? Harvesting? Are you feeling encouraged or discouraged about your opportunities to share your faith?

"Your work matters to God. Work is not something beneath God's dignity or concern, as some contend. Nor is work a game we play with non-Christians in order to accomplish a more important agenda...work is a major part of human life that God takes seriously."

– Douglas Sherman and William Hendricks,
Your Work Matters to God.

Chapter 10
Figuring Out Where We Fit in

1. Jot down a note or two about how you've struggled to feel like you belong
   * At work:
   * At church:
   * In your family:
   * Anywhere else:

2. Now mentally take a look around you in those same areas, do you see someone else who looks like they feel out-of-place?
   * At work:
   * At church:
   * In your family:
   * Anywhere else:

3. What can you do to remind yourself this week that you belong to God? What can you do to remind someone else this week that they belong to God too?

4. "No single piece of our mental world is to be hermetically sealed off from the rest, and there is not a square inch in the whole domain of our human existence over which Christ, who is Sovereign over all, does not cry: 'Mine!'"
   * How does Abraham Kuyper's quote encourage you? Does it help you to see the world as something Christ cares deeply about? How does that renewed vision, that Christ cares for every part of the human existence, motivate you?

Purposeful Resources Transforming Society

Visit Russell Media for our latest offerings:

www.russell-media.com

CPSIA information can be obtained at www.ICGtesting.com
Printed in the USA
LVOW04s1511071015

457324LV00016B/655/P

FEB 1 1 2016